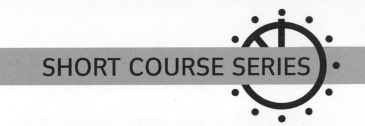
SHORT COURSE SERIES

Clockwise

elementary

Classbook

D1319355

Heather Potten &
Jonathan Potten

OXFORD
UNIVERSITY PRESS

Contents

LETTERS & NUMBERS

In this lesson
- The alphabet
- Dates
- Numbers

What do you know?
The alphabet

1 What do you know about the English alphabet?
1 How many letters has it got?
2 How many are vowels?
3 What do you call the other letters?
4 Which is the most common letter in English?
5 Which is the least common letter?

2 How do you pronounce the letters? Complete the columns.

a	b	f	i	o	q	r
	c					
	d					

> It's important to know how to pronounce the alphabet in English.

3 **In pairs.** Which letters are difficult to say? Test each other.
How do you say this letter?

4 **Against the clock** Say the alphabet round the class as quickly as you can. Can you do it in 20 seconds?

Speaking
Names and spelling

1 Make a list of the people in your class. Write their names in alphabetical order (by surname).
A Hello / Hi / Good evening. What's your name?
B I'm Jacques.
A And what's your surname?
B Breton.
A How do you spell that?
B B-R-E-T-O-N. And you? What's your name?
A Maria Alba.

Maria Alba
Jacques Breton

2 **In pairs.** Check the names you've got. Have you spelt them the same?

August

M	T	W	T	F	S	S
	1	2	3	4	5	6
7	8	9	10	11	12	13
14	15	16	17	18	19	20
21	22	23	24	25	26	27
28	29	30	31			

употреблять
применять
использовать

English in use

Dates

1 🕐 **Against the clock** `2 minutes` Write down the names of the months in English. Check your spelling in pairs.

2 In your country, which month is ...?
  1 a holiday month
  2 a hot month
  3 a wet month *aug*
  4 a depressing month *november*
  5 an important month for students *september*
  6 your favourite month *may*

3 **In groups.** Write down four dates when you do something special. Explain them to your group.

  9 May   *On the ninth of May we always go out because it's my sister's birthday.*

Numbers

1 Listen. Match the sentences you hear with the pictures.

2 Listen again and write down the missing numbers in each picture.

3 Make questions for the numbers.
  1 what's number ? your phone
  2 date ? the what's today
  3 old ? how you are
  4 ? mobile your number what's phone
  5 number house your what's ?
  6 ? birthday your when's

If you don't want to answer the question 'How old are you?', say 'It's a secret.'

Can you remember …?
- how to spell your name
- how to say the date
- how to say phone numbers

Practice p.76

4 **[○2]** Listen and check your ideas. Look at Tapescript 1.2 on *p.107* and practise the dialogues.

5 **In pairs.** Ask each other the questions in exercise 3.

Useful language

- When we say telephone numbers, 0 = *oh* and 22 = *double two*.
- What's the difference?

thirteen	thirty
fourteen	forty
fifteen	fifty

You can say '*thirty – that's three oh*' to make the difference clear.

- 126 = *one / a hundred and twenty-six*.

Speak out

You can answer lots of questions with letters, numbers, and dates. Play this game in groups of four. Use a coin to move. When you land on a square, answer the question. Make sure you say the letters and numbers correctly.

1 square HEADS

TAILS 2 squares

1 start — What's the date tomorrow?	2 — What are the vowels in English?	3 — When were you born?	4 — What's your phone number?
14 — What's your ID or passport number?	15 — How much money have you got on you?	16 — How do you spell your teacher's name?	5 — How many students are there in your class?
13 — What was the date last Friday?		7 — How do you pronounce 18 and 80?	6 — How do you spell the surname of the person on your left?
12 — What's your house or flat number?	11 — When does your credit card expire?	10 — When's your birthday?	9 — How many pages has this book got? / 8 — Have you got a mobile? What's the number?

02 COUNTRIES & PEOPLE

In this lesson
- Countries
- E-mail addresses
- *to be*, present and past

Speak for yourself

1 Look at the examples and write sentences about yourself with as much information as possible.

I'm from Switzerland.

*I'm from Switzerland, **from a small town called Baar**.*

*I'm from Switzerland, from a small town called Baar, **near Zürich**.*

I live in a flat.

*I live in a flat **in the centre of town**.*

*I live **with my wife and children** in a flat in the centre of town.*

- I'm from …
- I live …

2 **In groups.** Compare your sentences. Who has the longest? Ask questions for more information.

What's your wife's name?

How many children have you got?

Vocabulary

Countries

1 **In pairs.** Put these countries in the right stress group. Is *your* country in the list?

Brazil	Germany	Spain	Italy
Mexico	Russia	Hungary	Poland
France	Turkey	China	Japan
Portugal	Argentina	Sweden	Greece

O	Oo	oO	Ooo	ooOo
France Spain	Turkey Poland Russia	Brazil Japan	Mexico Germany	Argentina

2 Add another country to the table.

How do you pronounce _____ ?

How do you say these e-mail addresses? Which countries do the people live in?

monica@gold.com.br

elizabeth.brown@council.ru

hunterj@britcoun.gr

peter@sci.edu.au

msantos@esoterica.pt

Grammar

to be, present and past

1 Read Marzia's e-mail to Jim and his reply.

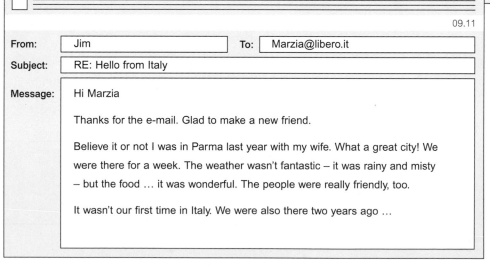

18.42

| From: | Marzia | To: | JimG@goweb.com |
| Subject: | Hello from Italy | | |

Message: Hi! My name's Marzia and I'm from Parma in Italy. I'm a nurse in an old people's home. It's not a bad job. The pay is terrible, but the hours are quite good. My boss is a monster, but never mind.

At the moment I'm living in a small flat in …

09.11

| From: | Jim | To: | Marzia@libero.it |
| Subject: | RE: Hello from Italy | | |

Message: Hi Marzia

Thanks for the e-mail. Glad to make a new friend.

Believe it or not I was in Parma last year with my wife. What a great city! We were there for a week. The weather wasn't fantastic – it was rainy and misty – but the food … it was wonderful. The people were really friendly, too.

It wasn't our first time in Italy. We were also there two years ago …

ago = in the past

Answer these questions:

Where were you | two hours **ago**?
| a month **ago**?
| exactly a week **ago**?

2 Close your books and write down three things you remember about Marzia and Jim.

3 **In groups.** Compare your lists and correct any mistakes.

4 Read about Marzia and Jim again. <u>Underline</u> the examples of *to be* in the present. (Circle) the examples of *to be* in the past.

to be, present and past

present	past
I'm	I was
I'm not	I wasn't
he's / she's / it's	he / she / it was
he / she / it isn't	he / she / it wasn't
you're / we're / they're	you / we / they were
you / we / they aren't	you / we / they weren't

Practice

1 Look at these sentences. Which must be in the past?
1   I _am_ a teacher.
2   I _was_ born in 1974.
3   I _was_ on holiday two weeks ago.
4   My birthday _is_ in July.
5   I _am_ married.
6   The weather _was_ sunny yesterday.
7   I _was_ in France last year.
8   I _am_ 50.
9   There _were_ ten students in my class.
10 The date tomorrow _is_ 1 March.

2 Now complete the sentences with *to be*, present or past. Make them true for you.
I'm a teacher.
or *I'm not a teacher. I'm a doctor.*

3 **In pairs.** Talk about your answers.

4 **In teams.** Write down the names of six famous people, three dead and three alive. Ask the other teams where they are from.
A Where's Ronaldo from?
B (He's from) Brazil.
A Where was Mozart from?
B (He was from) Austria.

Speak out

1 Write a short e-mail about yourself.

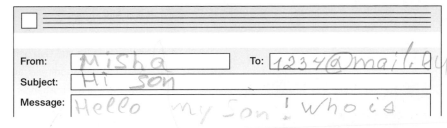

From:	Misha	To:	1234@mail.by
Subject:	Hi son		
Message:	Hello my son! Who is		

2 **In pairs.** Read each other's e-mails.

3 **In groups.** Tell the group about your partner. Don't look at their e-mail. How much can you remember?

Can you remember …?
• five countries and nationalities
• how to say e-mail addresses
• the past of *to be*
Practice p.77

03
FRIENDS & RELATIONS

In this lesson
- Family vocabulary
- Home vocabulary
- *have got / has got*
- Talking about where people live

My brother's name = the name of my brother

Vocabulary challenge

1 Look at these words. What's the difference between the words in red, blue, and green?

father   daughter   niece   grandfather   child
spouse   wife   ex-wife   cousin   mother-in-law
parent   grandson   uncle   boyfriend   brother

2 **In pairs.** Look at the red and blue words. What's the other word in the pair? Test each other.

   A Father.   *B* Mother ... Wife.   *A* Husband.

3 **In groups.** Choose three of your relations and tell each other something about them.

   My brother's name is David, and he's married with three children.

Grammar

have got / has got

1 Are these sentences true (✓) or false (✗) for you? Compare your ideas.

when I was young	now
I lived in a large house.	I live in a large city.
It was in a village.	I live on my own.
There were three bedrooms.	My house / flat has got central heating.
There was no electricity.	My house / flat has a beautiful view.

2 Read about Rita and her family. Which of the sentences in exercise 1 are true for her?

   I lived in a large house. ✗ *She lived in a small house.*

My mother's house is in the village of Kardiani. The house is about 100 years old. My family is big – six brothers and sisters and my mother (my father died when I was 12). It was a small house for seven people. It's got a big living room and two bedrooms. We slept in the bedrooms and the living room. The bathroom was, and still is, outside. It was so cold in winter! Now, I live in my husband's village. I'm near my mother, but not too near! It's a new house, and it's got lots of space, a beautiful kitchen, and a large balcony. We've got heating (which my mother's house hasn't) and a large, comfortable bathroom inside! Unfortunately, we haven't got a very good view. There's another house opposite us, so we can't see the mountains.

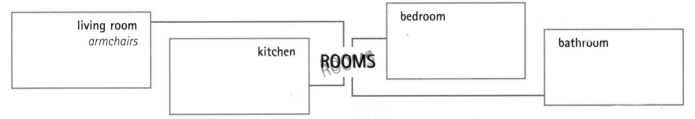

My daughter, Eleni, left the island two years ago to find a job. She lives in Athens and rents a small flat in one of the suburbs. It's a good area, but very busy and noisy. She lives alone, but her boyfriend lives nearby. The flat is on the top floor and on a clear day you can see the Acropolis! She hasn't got air-conditioning, so it's very hot in summer. That's why she comes home when she can ...

3 Against the clock `3 minutes` Read the texts again and find as many rooms and parts of a house as you can.

4 Look at this spidergram. Can you put three things in each room?

| living room | | | bedroom | |
| *armchairs* | kitchen | **ROOMS** | | bathroom |

5 Look back at the text. How many examples of *have got / has got* can you find? How many are negative?

have got / has got

| I you we they | ➕ | 've got haven't got | | Have _____ got ...? | ➡ | Yes, _____ have. No, _____ haven't. |
| he she it | ➕ | 's got hasn't got | | Has _____ got ...? | ➡ | Yes, _____ has. No, _____ hasn't. |

Practice

1 Look at the grammar box and make these sentences true for you.
  1 I _have_ a pet.
  2 I _have_ a big family.
  3 My bedroom _has_ an en suite bathroom.
  4 My parents _____ a house in the country.
  5 My car _____ air-conditioning.
  6 My best friend _____ dark hair and brown eyes.

2 Put these words in the right order to make questions.
  1 brothers got many have how and sisters you ?
  2 house your got air-conditioning has ?
  3 a you player got CD have ?
  4 you nephews got and any have nieces ?
  5 free much time have how you got ?
  6 you have flat house or got a a ?

3 In pairs. Ask and answer the questions.

English in use
Where do you live?

1 [○1] Listen to Diana and Shawn talking about where they live. Complete the table.

	Diana	Shawn
where	*a village near Oxford*	
who with		
rooms		
favourite room		*living room*

2 Who says what? Put **D** (Diana) or **S** (Shawn) beside each phrase.

1 about 80 years old   *D*
2 on the third floor
3 it's pretty big
4 upstairs
5 there are three bedrooms
6 a view of the garden
7 my favorite room's
8 that's where I watch TV

3 Listen to the recording again and check. Practise saying the phrases.

4 What can you remember? Try to complete these sentences. Check in Tapescript 3.1.

Diana

1 I live in a _____ in a _____ near Oxford.
2 It's about _____ years old and made of _____ .
3 Upstairs there are three _____ and two _____ .
4 Our bedroom has a view of the _____ and the _____ beyond.

Shawn

5 My apartment's on the _____ floor of an old _____ house.
6 It's _____ big for _____ _____ .
7 My favorite room's the _____ . That's where I _____ TV and _____ to music.
8 It's also where the _____ is – it gets hot in Boston.

5 Write a short description of your house / flat, using the phrases above for ideas.

British English	American English
flat	*apartment*
favourite	*favorite*

Can you remember …?
- six relations
- five rooms in a house
- three things about Diana and Shawn's homes

Practice p.78

Speak out

1 Think of friends or members of your family who live in these places. If you can, write one name for each.

(in the same house as me) (in the same neighbourhood as me) (in the same village / town / city) (in the same part of the country) (in a different part of the country) (in another country)

2 **In groups / pairs.** Choose one or two of the people. Say who they are, and describe where they live. Give as much detail as you can, and try to use words and phrases from this lesson.

04
LIFE & ROUTINE

In this lesson
- Daily routine vocabulary
- The present simple
- Talking about routines

What do you know?

1 Make as many sentences as you can.
I get the bus to work.

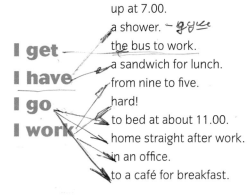

I get
I have
I go
I work

up at 7.00.
a shower. ～샤워
the bus to work.
a sandwich for lunch.
from nine to five.
hard!
to bed at about 11.00.
home straight after work.
in an office.
to a café for breakfast.

2 Tick (✓) the sentences that are true for you.

3 **In groups.** Compare your ideas.

Vocabulary

Daily routines

1 **Against the clock** 3 minutes Look at these words. Can you think of one verb that goes with each?

have a sandwich   *go* by bike   *work* in an office

sandwich	TV	shower	dinner
bike	friends	bus	gym
office	lunch	restaurant	coffee
paper	café	bed	bath

2 1 Listen to these three people talking about their daily routine. Complete the gaps. Which expressions in exercise 1 do they use?

1 I usually __*get up*__ at about 6.30. I just _____ for breakfast.
I _____ to work. If I'm late I _____ , which is a bit expensive.
My wife _____ , she likes to keep fit.

2 I always _____ at lunchtimes, about 12.30 or 12.45. I _____ there too, and I often _____ for lunch.

3 I _____ at around 6.00 and maybe _____ for a drink. I don't _____ , too much to do, and I never _____ before midnight.

How do you say
_____ (in English)?

3 What times do these clocks say? Use these words.

o'clock

quarter past / to

half past

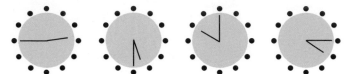

Grammar

Present simple

1 Complete the sentences with the words in the box.

work	takes	do	don't like
works	does	doesn't drink	don't watch
go	live	do	
goes	read	do	

1   Mr Yorke _____ in a secondary school in London.
2   Which newspaper _____ you _____ ?
3   Alison and Nick _____ to work by bus. They _____ _____ driving.
4   Sally _____ _____ coffee.
5   The 26 bus _____ you straight to the city centre.
6   What _____ he _____ ?
7   They never _____ at the weekend.
8   She _____ home at 5.00.
9   Where _____ your parents _____ ?
10 I _____ _____ a lot of TV.

2 In pairs. Check your answers together.

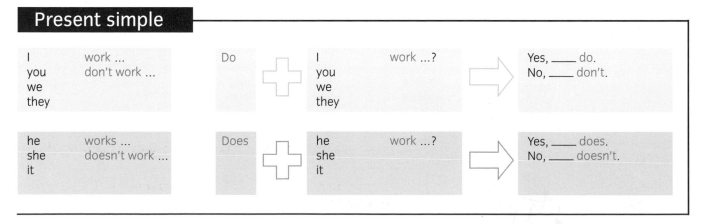

Present simple				
I you we they	work ... don't work ...	Do	I you we they	work ...?	Yes, ____ do. No, ____ don't.
he she it	works ... doesn't work ...	Does	he she it	work ...?	Yes, ____ does. No, ____ doesn't.

Practice

1 Correct the verbs in these sentences.

1 I am phone her every day.
   I phone her every day.
2 We not work at the weekend.
3 How you get home?
4 I'm start work at nine o'clock.
5 She doesn't drives to work.
6 They like living in the United States?
7 Are you always have a sandwich for lunch?
8 Do this bus go to the city centre?

2 Write five sentences with *every* about things you or other people do.

3 In pairs. Read these tips for getting a good night's sleep. Tell your partner what you do and don't do.
I lock all my doors, but I don't listen to music.

> You can use *every* with periods of time.
>
> *He has a cigarette **every ten minutes**.*
> *She has a coffee **every morning**.*
> *We go to London **every weekend**.*
> *They visit me **every year**.*

SLEEP WELL

Get into a routine – go to bed at the same time every day.

Go to bed before midnight.

Never eat or work in bed.

Make sure you lock all your doors.

Always leave a window open.

Listen to relaxing music before you go to bed.

Never have a pet in the bedroom with you.

Have a bath before you go to bed.

Make sure the room is dark.

Read a book for ten minutes – but not a horror story.

Can you remember ...?
- six phrases to describe your daily routine
- how to tell the time
- when to use *-s* with a verb

Practice p.80

Speak out

1 In pairs. Tell your partner about your routine. Use as many words from this lesson as you can.

2 In groups. Tell the group about your partner's routine. Whose is the most interesting or unusual?

> Every week is exactly the same. Sometimes I feel like a robot.
> Is every week the same for you? Do you sometimes feel like a robot too?

05
PEOPLE & PLACES

In this lesson

- Describing people and places
- Present simple third person
- Adverbs of frequency

Vocabulary challenge

1 Put these adjectives in the right box (some go in more than one).

freezing	friendly	relaxed	sunny
delicious	horrible	cheap	hot
salty	interesting	caring	boring
expensive	wet	tasty	beautiful

2 **In groups.** Which of the adjectives could describe the people, food, and weather in your country?

English in use
Describing your life

1  **Against the clock** [1 minute] Read about Becky and Ruth, two British women working abroad. What are their jobs? Do you think they enjoy what they do?

Mongolia

Routine

I often wake up with bright sunshine coming through my bedroom window – the best way to start the day! I start work at nine o'clock and finish at six. I teach university students for four hours a day, and spend the rest of my time planning classes and preparing exams with colleagues.

Good things

My work's very interesting – I never know what will happen next. All the

Becky

people I work with are extremely friendly, caring, and good fun. They're always worried about my flat, my health, my eating habits, and my social life! And I love the weather – Mongolia is called 'the land of blue sky', and it almost never rains.

Bad things

The cold and the distances – Mongolia is a long way from anywhere else, and I only see my friends once a year. The temperature is sometimes around −20°C in winter, it's really freezing. Horse's milk and salty tea are popular drinks, but not with me!

Solomon Islands

Routine

Classes start at 7.30 a.m. We teach in leaf hut classrooms which badly need repairing. There aren't enough chairs and desks, so students who arrive late sit three or four to a desk. There's usually a lovely breeze coming from the sea 100 metres away. I finish at about 3.00, and the rest of the day is my own. I hardly ever work at weekends.

Good things

The beautiful sunny mornings. The tranquillity and the relaxed

Ruth

atmosphere. The friendly people who always say hello, and the kids with smiling faces and orange-blonde hair. And the local family that I live with.

Bad things

The insects, the waiting, and the heat. It's usually very, very wet between January and April. Imported food is expensive, and I'm a bit bored with fish, rice, and sweet potato ...

2 Read the texts again, then close your books. Can you remember the good and bad things about each place?

3 Are these sentences probably about Becky or Ruth? How do you know?

1 Every Sunday she washes her clothes and dries them on the beach.
2 She teaches children.
3 She studies Chinese and Russian in the evening.
4 She goes for a swim when she finishes work.
5 She has fresh fruit for breakfast.
6 She wears three jumpers to work in winter.
7 She goes out with her colleagues a lot.
8 She always takes malaria tablets.
9 She misses her friends.
10 She doesn't have an umbrella.

Present simple spelling – *he / she / it*

| wash
teach
miss
go | + *es* | → | washes
teaches
misses
goes | study
dry | y + *ies* | → | studies
dries |

4 Study the spelling box. How many examples can you find in the sentences in exercise 3?

5 Now complete these sentences. Make sure you put each verb in the correct form.

| dry | wash | miss | study | go |

1 He _____ his mother a lot.
2 They _____ to church every Sunday.
3 As my hair is so short, it _____ very quickly.
4 I _____ hard but I always fail tests and exams. It's nerves.
5 She _____ her clothes in the river. Their house doesn't have running water.

6 Listen to these five sentences and write down the verb.

1 How is the verb pronounced?
2 Can you remember the complete sentences? Listen again and check.

Grammar

Adverbs of frequency

1 Test your memory. Complete these sentences about Becky and Ruth.

usually	never	sometimes
always	often	hardly ever

1 I _____ wake up with bright sunshine coming through the window.
2 They're _____ worried about my eating habits and my social life.
3 It almost _____ rains.
4 The temperature is _____ around −20°C in winter.
5 I _____ work at weekends.
6 It's _____ very wet between January and April.

2 Can you put the adverbs in exercise 1 in order?

3 Tick (✓) the sentences that are true for you.
1 I always have a cup of tea first thing in the morning. ✓
2 I sometimes go to the beach at the weekend. ✓
3 I hardly ever go to the theatre. ✓
4 I usually wear a tie. ✓
5 I sometimes go out in the evening. ✓
6 I always buy expensive clothes. ✓
7 At weekends I often sit around and do nothing. ✓
8 I never eat chips. ✓

4 Make the other sentences true by changing the adverb of frequency.
*I **never** have a cup of tea first thing in the morning.*

5 **In pairs.** Tell each other your sentences. Ask more questions.
A *I never have a cup of tea first thing in the morning.*
B *What do you have?*

100%	always
	_____
	_____
	_____
	_____
0%	never

Can you remember …?
- four adjectives to describe weather
- when to use -es with a verb
- six adverbs of frequency

Practice p.82

Speak out

1 Look back at the texts about Becky and Ruth. Copy the table and write sentences about a typical English language teacher from abroad living in your country. Try to use adverbs of frequency.

Routine	Good things 😊	Bad things 😞
what they do every day	people, weather, language, food, money, etc.	
They often work in the evenings.		*They sometimes have problems with the language.*

2 **In groups.** Compare your ideas.

06
JOBS & WORK

In this lesson
- Jobs and occupations
- Job adverts
- Talking about what you do

> What does
> ———— mean?

Speak for yourself

1 Tick (✓) the things you think are important in a job.

- [ ] a good salary
- [ ] working alone
- [ ] lots of travel
- [ ] long holidays
- [ ] working outdoors
- [ ] working at home
- [ ] an interesting routine
- [ ] working in a team
- [ ] a company car
- [ ] being the boss
- [ ] working in an office
- [ ] working near home

2 In pairs. Tell your partner what you think is important and what you like / don't like.

I think a good salary is important, and I like working in a team.

Vocabulary
Occupations

> *a* + consonant
> *I'm a student.*
> *an* + vowel
> *I'm an architect.*

1 Can you answer this question in two ways?

> What do you do?

> 1 *I'm a student.*
> 2 *I go to the University of Prague.*

> 1 *I'm a bank clerk.*
> 2 *I work for a German bank.*

 2 Against the clock `2 minutes` Match these jobs to the pictures.

lawyer	shop assistant	photographer	secretary
teacher	computer programmer	bus driver	journalist
nurse	builder		

3 Now match six of the jobs with these sentences.

1 I spend my whole day typing letters – it's a bit boring.

2 I like looking after people, but I don't earn much.

3 I hate the traffic.

4 I work for a small local paper.

5 I work in a secondary school.

6 I sometimes work on Sundays before Christmas.

4 Write your own sentences for the other four jobs.

 5 Listen to these three dialogues and write down the answers.

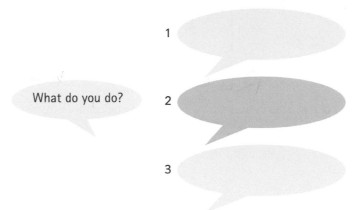

What do you do?

1

2

3

6 In pairs. Notice the way the words join together. Practise saying them in the same way.

A What do you do?

B I'm a doctor.

7 In groups. Think of two people you know. Can you explain what they do?

English in use
Job adverts

1 Match the beginnings and ends of the sentences.

1	If you wear good clothes,	you get **a degree**.
2	If you have done a job before,	you are **motivated**.
3	If you speak and listen well,	you are **smart**.
4	If you want to do well in a job,	you have good **communication skills**.
5	If you study at university,	you are **experienced**.
6	If you earn a lot of money,	you have **a high salary**.

advertisement = advert = ad

2 Look at the job adverts on the next page.

1 How many different jobs are advertised?

2 Match the jobs with the words in exercise 1.

3 What is 'blue'?

4 Which job needs most experience?

5 What is the minimum salary for the English Lecturer?

6 How can you contact Maria Philips?

blue

the following positions are now available in glasgow and edinburgh

waiters, waitresses, bar servers

you should be smart and motivated

chefs

you should have at least two years' experience – salary excellent

if you are interested, please contact steve on 0131 921 1221

Langside College Exeter

English Lecturer
£15,885 to £23,305

Applicants should have a degree in English, a teaching qualification, and three years' experience in an institute of higher education. Good communication skills are essential.

For further details contact:
Maria Philips, Langside College,
50 Prospect Road, Exeter, EX6 3DE
philipsm@langside.ac.uk
direct line 01392 345777

Speak out

1 Think about your job or a job you'd like to have.
2 Make notes on the qualities and qualifications needed for your job. Try to use language from the **English in use** section.

qualities	qualifications

How do you say _____ (in English)?

patient   BA   teaching qualifications
a degree   experienced   training
motivated   university   energetic   MSc
college   smart

Can you remember ...?
- three things that you think are important in a job
- another way to say *What's your job?*
- three things you need to get a good job

Practice p.83

3 **In groups.** Tell each other about your job / future job.

For my (future) job I need | *a degree.*
to be smart.

07
LOVE & HATE

In this lesson

- Activities vocabulary
- Likes and dislikes
- *-ing* forms

What do you know?

1 Are these activities indoor or outdoor? Put them in the right column. Which can go in both columns?

watching TV	going to the cinema	jogging
playing (football)	reading the paper	clubbing
doing nothing	surfing the Net	hill-walking
snowboarding	window shopping	eating out

indoor	outdoor
watching TV	

2 Think of two more indoor and outdoor activities. Compare your ideas.

Grammar

Likes and dislikes

 1 **Against the clock** `1 minute` Memorize the activities above. Then cover them.

2 What do you like doing? Put all the activities you remember in these shapes.

I love _____

I really like / enjoy _____

I don't mind / I quite like _____

I don't like _____ much

I hate / can't stand _____

3 **In pairs.** Compare your likes and dislikes.

A I love surfing the Net.

B I don't like it much – it's sometimes very slow.

Likes and dislikes

I love I (really) like I enjoy I quite like I don't like I hate I can't stand		noun ⇒	I love old films.
		-ing ⇒	I hate working on Saturdays.

Do you like _____?
Yes, I do.
Yes, I love it / them.
It's OK.
No, I don't.
Not really.
Not much.

4 Look at these *-ing* forms. What are the spelling rules?

cook   cooking
practise   practising
run   running

 5 **Against the clock** `1 minute` What are the *-ing* forms of these verbs?

sit	sleep	use	come	try	win

Practice

1 Read about these people. Which person is most like you? Why?

Alex SECRETARY   *She likes*
01 shopping **02** her dog Strudel
03 triathlon **04** black and white films
05 being at home

Karen ACCOUNTANT   *She likes*
01 eating outside in summer
02 travelling **03** Italian food
04 flip flops **05** swimming in the sea

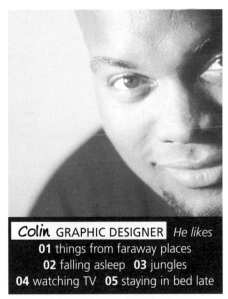

Colin GRAPHIC DESIGNER   *He likes*
01 things from faraway places
02 falling asleep **03** jungles
04 watching TV **05** staying in bed late

2 Which person do you think likes these things? How do you know?

cycling	watching videos	buying Christmas presents
pasta	expensive shoes	going to the beach
pets	comfortable beds	tropical countries

 3 Listen to these sentences and <u>underline</u> the stressed word or words. Practise saying them in the same way.

1 I <u>love</u> eating out at the weekend.

2 I can't stand doing nothing.

3 I really like watching TV in the evenings.

4 I quite like clubbing.

5 I hate reading the paper.

2

4 Listen and complete the gaps.

1 I love _____ ... the sea, the fresh air ...
2 Sometimes I just like _____ around , _____ nothing.
3 I _____ noisy pubs. I can never hear people.
4 I quite enjoy _____ alone. I don't always need company.
5 I hate _____ when it's still dark.
6 I quite like _____ football on the box, but I prefer _____ .
7 I _____ gardening. It hurts my back.
8 I _____ the weather here. It's so depressing.

EXPAND your vocabulary

Learn words to talk about what you're interested in or what you enjoy.
Think of something you like doing and find five new words to talk about it.

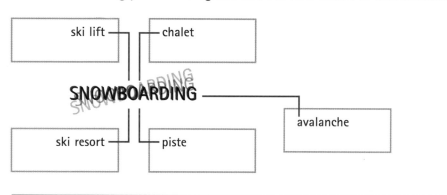

How do you say _____ (in English)?

Speak out

1 Read this short poem.

> I like playing tennis
> I like walking
> I like going swimming
> but
> I don't like one thing:
> smoking.

2 In groups. Complete this poem about your group. Ask each other questions to find out three things you all like, and one thing that nobody likes.

> We _____
> We _____
> We _____
> but
> We _____ one thing:
> _____ .

Can you remember ...?
• four indoor activitites
• how to spell *-ing* forms
• five ways to talk about likes and dislikes
Practice p.85

3 Read your poems to the class. Is there anything that nobody likes?

08
ZOOS & BARS

In this lesson

- Entertainment vocabulary
- Understanding city guides
- Describing what's on in your town

You see | **a film** or **movie** in a cinema.
| **a play** in a theatre.
| **an exhibition** in a museum.

I like going to **the** cinema / **the** theatre.

but I like going to **bars**.

Vocabulary challenge

1 Match the beginnings and endings of these places and label the pictures.

m	inema
c	useum
t	afé
r	rt gallery
a	lub
c	heatre
c	oo
z	ar
b	estaurant

2 ⏱ **Against the clock** `3 minutes` **In pairs.**
Think of two things you associate with each place.

cinema   *film, popcorn*

3 Test another pair. Can they guess the place from your words?

A film, popcorn
B cinema

4 In groups. Which places do you like going to? Why? How often do you go? Use these words.

once		a week
twice	✚	a month
three times		a year

I like going to clubs because I love dancing. I go once or twice a week.

English in use
Things to do

1 Complete the definitions with the words in the box. Use a dictionary to help you.

concessions
a matinée
admission
noon
a booking fee
subtitles

	is how much you pay to get in.
	is money you have to pay to book tickets.
	is an afternoon show in the cinema or the theatre.
	are the words at the bottom of the picture on TV or in the cinema.
	are cheaper tickets for students, etc.
	is the same as 12.00 midday.

2 Match these abbreviations and words.

Mon	performance
concs	matinée
adm	Street
hols	Monday
perf	admission
mat	holidays
Rd	concessions
St	Road

Time Out is a magazine which tells you what's on in London.

3 Read the extracts from *Time Out*. Which things do you think you would enjoy?

Natural History Museum
020 79389123

Cromwell Rd SW7 ⊖ South Kensington. Mon–Sat 10am–5.50pm, Sun 11am–5.50pm. Adults £6.50, children (0–16) free, concs £3.50; free adm Mon–Fri 4.30–5.50pm, Sat, Sun, and Bank Hols 5–5.50pm.

Our turning world
exhibition of 350 photographs by Magnum photographers Barbican 020 75889023 → Oct 12; Mon–Sat 10am–6pm, Weds until 8pm, Sun noon–6pm. £6, concs £4.

ABC Shaftesbury Avenue W1
020 7836 6279, Visa M'Card 020 8795 6403 subject to booking fee

⊖Tottenham Ct Rd, admission £6.50 (Mon £4.30, Tue–Fri perfs before 5.00pm £4.30); students, children, senior citizens £4.30. Seats: screen 1–615, screen 2–581.

► **East is East** (15) Progs 1.30, 3.50, 6.20 (not Thur), 8.50
► **Fast Food** (18) Progs 1.10, 3.30, 6.10, 8.30
► **Time Regained** (18) subtitles, Progs 1.10, 4.30, 7.50

The Breakfast Club
Arch 66 Goding St. SE11 6.30am–1pm, £5 no concs, the fun continues when everyone else has gone home to bed, with Lisa Reds, Roosta and Stormin D.

Basketball
London Leopards v London Towers, Brentwood Centre. 01277 215151. Admission £7.00 (£5.00 children), Wed. 2 Nov 7.30pm. All tickets sold.

Romeo and Juliet
Westminster Theatre 020 78340283, 12 Palace St SW1 ⊖ Victoria → Sat 5 Nov last perf. Mon–Sat 7.30, Wed, Thur & Sat Mat 3.00pm. £15, £10 concs. Runs 2h10.

4 In pairs. Divide into **A** and **B** and answer the questions. Then compare and explain your answers.

A

1	The Natural History Museum opens at 10.00 every day.	T/F
2	Students can get into the photography exhibition for £4.	T/F
3	The ABC cinema has seating for over 1,000 people.	T/F
4	If you book tickets at the ABC by phone, you have to pay extra.	T/F
5	Which film isn't in English?	_____
6	Which event has no tickets left?	_____
7	What's the ABC cinema credit card booking number?	_____
8	How much is admission to the Breakfast Club?	_____

B

1	There are four matinée performances of *Romeo and Juliet*.	T/F
2	All tickets for the basketball are £7.	T/F
3	You can't go to the photography exhibition on Sunday mornings.	T/F
4	The Breakfast Club is a restaurant.	T/F
5	When can you get into the Natural History Museum free at weekends?	_____
6	What time does the photography exhibition open on Sunday?	_____
7	Which place has no special prices?	_____
8	How long is the performance of *Romeo and Juliet*?	_____

5 Write questions for these answers. Use the words in (brackets).

1 020 79389123.   (What's)
   What's the phone number of the Natural History Museum?
2 6.30 a.m.   (What time)
3 October 12.   (When)
4 £7.   (How much)
5 020 78340283.   (What's)
6 350.   (How many)

Speak out

1 Take five minutes to think about your home town or a city you know. What entertainments and activities are there? Look at the places in this lesson for ideas and make a list.

2 In pairs, A and B.

A Tell your partner what's on.
   There's a cinema with international films (every Friday).
   There's an excellent Japanese restaurant in the city centre.
   Their speciality is ...

B Listen to your partner and decide what sounds interesting.
   The cinema sounds interesting.
   I like the sound of the Japanese restaurant.

3 Then change round. **B** tell **A** what's on.

Can you remember ...?
- six places to go to in towns or cities
- how to use *once* and *twice*
- what *subtitles*, *noon*, and *booking fee* mean

Practice *p.86*

In this lesson

- Places in a town / city
- Asking where places are
- Prepositions

Speak for yourself

1 Look at this student's map of Kinshi, a suburb of Tokyo. Can you find these places?

- two places to eat
- two places to drink
- an important road
- a bus stop and a train station

- somewhere to go shopping
- somewhere to see films
- a park
- where the student lives

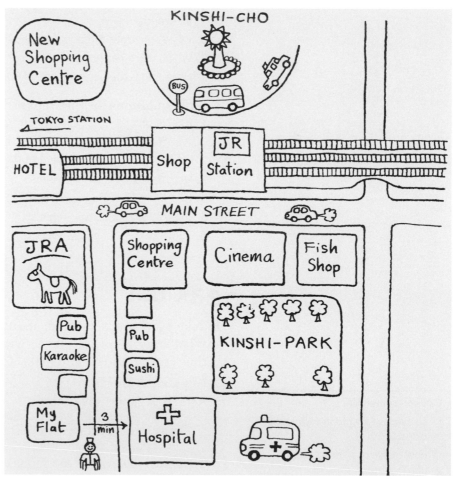

2 Against the clock `3 minutes` Draw a map of the centre of your home town. Include some of the places above if you can.

3 In pairs. Compare your maps. Describe them, and ask questions.

How do you get to the centre?

How long does it take you to get there?

Where do you work / study?

How often do you go to the centre? Why?

English in use
Saying where things are

1 Look at the map. How many different words can you find? Make an alphabetical list.

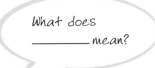

What does
_____ mean?

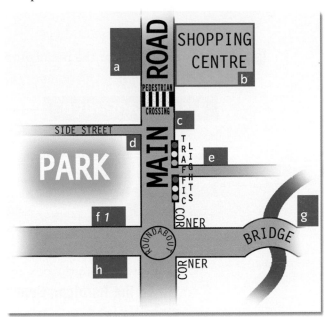

 2 Now listen and mark these places on the map.

1 museum	3 post office	5 Italian restaurant	7 chemist's
2 Chinese restaurant	4 art gallery	6 cinema	8 supermarket

3 What did the second people say? Complete these sentences with the correct preposition.

1 Yeah, it's _____ the roundabout.
2 Yes, it's _____ that side street, _____ the traffic lights.
3 Yes, there's one just down there, _____ the lights and the shopping centre.
4 Yes, it's there, _____ the corner.
5 Yes, keep going, it's _____ the bridge.
6 Do you know the museum? It's _____ there.
7 Yes, there's one _____ that big shopping centre.
8 Yes, it's _____ this main road, _____ the left.

4 Listen again and check.

Prepositions

1 Match the prepositions with the diagrams.

near	opposite
on	next to
between	in

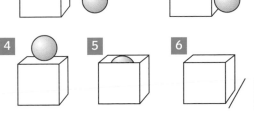

2 🕐 **Against the clock** [2 minutes] How many sentences can you make about Kinshi with the prepositions?
The hotel is near the station.

Practice

A *Where's the bus station?*

B *Could you tell me where the bus station is?*

A *Excuse me, is there a post office near here?*

B *Is there a post office?*

1 Look at these questions. Which do you think are more polite?

 2 Listen and repeat the polite questions. Make sure you stress the place you want to go.

Useful language

How do I get to (the) _____ ?

Could you tell me how to get to (the) _____ , please?

Could you tell me where (the) _____ is, please?

Excuse me, is (the) _____ near here?

Is this the way to (the) _____ , please?

3 **In pairs, A and B. A** point to one of these places in London, **B** ask a polite question from the box above.

the Barbican Centre

the National Gallery   Paddington Station

Victoria Coach Station   the Museum of the Moving Image

the Westminster Theatre   the Tate Gallery

Speak out

1 Look at this map. Can you pronounce the names of the streets?

Can you remember ...?

* how to ask where places are
* prepositions to describe position
* the difference between a *main road* and a *side street*

Practice p.87

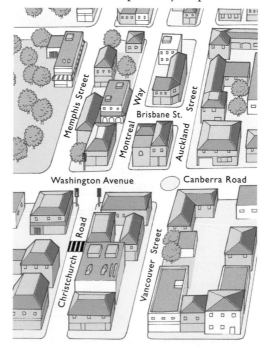

2 **In pairs, A and B. A** look at the map on *p.105*. **B** look at the map on *p.106*.

10
GOOD & BAD

In this lesson

- Adjectives for *good* and *bad*
- Giving your opinion
- *quite, really, absolutely*

3 Oscar nominations

By the River

**A film by Manolo Han
Now showing at ABCs
round the country**

John Blake
retrospective

**60 years of painting and sculpture
Hogg Gallery, W1**

For the best pizzas north of Naples
PIZZERIA LA QUERCIA

**9 Highton Road
Manchester**

Listening challenge

1 Look at these adverts. What are they for?

Oriente de Cuba

featuring some of the greatest
names in Cuban Music

Royal Queen's Hall
020 79904241

'The best novel of
the 21st century'

CHINA GREEN

by Helen K. Shapiro
Country Press

2 🔘1 Listen to these six people. Which advert are they talking about?
How do you know?

Vocabulary
Opinion adjectives

1 Match the words to the number of stars.

not bad	really good	brilliant	nothing special	terrible

	★
	★★
not bad	★★★
	★★★★
	★★★★★

2 **Against the clock** 3 minutes Look at these words and phrases and put
them in the chart. Use a dictionary if you want.

great	fantastic	awful	not very good
disappointing	excellent	very good	OK

3 **In pairs.** Practise saying the adjectives from exercises 1 and 2. Which
have two or more syllables? Which syllable is stressed?

disappointing = dis + a + **ppoin** + ting

English in use
Giving your opinion

1 In groups of three, A, B, and C. Here are three opinions of the James Bond film *The World Is Not Enough.* **A** read Adam's opinion, **B** read Natalie's, **C** read James's. Complete your part of the table.

	Adam	Natalie	James
What do they like in the film?			
What do they dislike in the film?			
What positive adjectives do they use?			
What negative adjectives do they use?			

Adam Jones

48, chartered accountant

Why? There were good reviews in the papers.
Well? Excellent entertainment. I still think Sean Connery was the best Bond, but Pierce Brosnan is terrific, too! Robert Carlyle is a bit disappointing as the bad guy, though.
Best bit? The scene at the beginning when Pierce Brosnan jumps out of the window in Bilbao. Very exciting.

Natalie French

22, police constable

Why? It was my boyfriend's idea.
Well? Quite good. Bond films are usually terrible but it was better than I expected. Pierce Brosnan's nice, and I really like Sophie Marceau – she's a brilliant baddie.
Best bit? The scene when Brosnan and Marceau are skiing in the mountains.

James Martin

30, teacher

Why? I love Bond movies.
Well? Nothing special. The action scenes are like some of the older Bond films, and not as exciting. It's quite shocking when Bond kills a woman – he's usually such a gentleman!
Best bit? The chase with the speed boats in the Thames. Bond's boat is really cool.

Why? = Why did you go to see the film?

Well? = Well, what do you think of the film?

Best bit? = What was the best part?

---

2 Cover the texts. Ask each other questions, and complete the rest of the table.
B What does Adam like in the film?
A Pierce Brosnan and the scene at the beginning.

3 How many stars (★ ★★ ★★★ ★★★★ ★★★★★) do you think each person gives the film?

Useful language

Look at the opinions again. Find three words that we can use before adjectives to change their meaning. Which two are strongest?

q_____   r_____   v_____

You can use *absolutely* to give very strong opinions using ★★★★★ or ★ words.

Positive ★★★★★	It was absolutely	fantastic. great.
Negative ★	It was absolutely	terrible. awful.

Practice

1 Listen to these people giving their opinions. Can you complete the sentences?

    1 **A** What did you think of the book?
        B It was _____ _____ .
    2 **A** How was the film?
        B I thought it was _____ .
    3 **A** What was the restaurant like last night?
        B The food was _____ _____ .
    4 **A** How was that exhibition you went to?
        B It was _____ _____ .
    5 **A** How was the book?
        B I thought it was _____ .
    6 **A** What was the concert like?
        B It was _____ _____ .

2 Listen to the answers again and mark the main stresses. Practise saying the sentences.

    It was really good.

3 Look at this dialogue. Can you think of three possible questions for **B**? Check your ideas in exercise 1.

    A I went to that new Japanese restaurant last night.
    B _____ ?
    A It wasn't bad – a bit expensive, but the food was quite good.

4 **In pairs.** Make similar dialogues with this information.
   - that **new club** last night / absolutely awful / décor cheap / music terrible
   - an **art exhibition** yesterday / not very good / paintings OK / photos nothing special
   - that **new café** this morning / excellent / building beautiful / coffee fantastic

5 **In groups.** Think of two things you did last week. Did you enjoy them? Can you explain why / why not?

Can you remember ...?
- three positive and three negative adjectives
- ... and how to pronounce them
- how to use *absolutely*

Practice p.89

Speak out

1 On four separate pieces of paper write the names of:

    • **a famous actor**

    • **a film**

    • **a singer / musician**

    • **a sports personality**

Make sure you choose two that you like and two that you *don't* like.

2 **In groups.** Put all your pieces of paper together. Choose one and talk about your opinions. Try to use adjectives from this lesson, and *very, really, quite,* and *absolutely*. Do you all agree?

    A I really like Kevin Spacey. He's absolutely fantastic.
    B I don't agree. I think he's really boring.

To say what you think, use:
I agree.
I don't agree. I think ...

11
OUT & ABOUT

In this lesson

- Making plans
- Present continuous for plans
- Spelling *-ing* forms

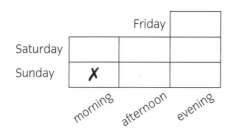

	morning	afternoon	evening
Friday			
Saturday			
Sunday	✗		

Speak for yourself

1 Most of us like the weekend. But what is your favourite time and why? Put an ✗ in the chart and write a sentence.

My favourite time is Sunday morning because I can sleep late and read the paper in bed.

2 **In groups.** Compare your ideas. Is anybody the same?

3 How often do you do something different for the weekend? What do you do?

Grammar
Present continuous for plans

1 **In groups.** Put the boxes in order to make two conversations, a–h and 1–8.

a
1	What are you doing this weekend?

Absolutely. Well, have a great time. And see you on Monday.

Yeah, but we're not staying anywhere very nice, I don't think. But anything's OK for £69!

Oh, nothing much. Shopping, maybe, and a bit of telly.

Well, we're driving so we can pick you up. About 7.45?

We're going to Paris! Jane saw a special offer, £69 all in, so we thought let's go for it.

Fantastic! When are you leaving?

That sounds great – where are you going?

And is everything included? Accommodation and everything?

Well, if you feel like it, Bella and I are going out for dinner on Saturday, and you'd be more than welcome to come.

That Italian place, Umberto's. The food's really excellent. We're meeting Keith there at 8.00. Do you know where it is?

We're getting the train on Friday evening, at 7.30.

No, I don't actually.

h
8	OK. See you then.

34

2 Listen and check your answers.

3 Cover the conversations. Can you complete these sentences?
1 What _____ this weekend?
2 Bella and I _____ for dinner on Saturday.
3 We _____ Keith there at 8.00.
4 We _____ so we can pick you up.
5 We _____ anywhere very nice.

Present continuous

Form

| I'm
I'm not
he's / she's / it's
he / she / it isn't
we're / you're / they're
we / you / they aren't |  | verb *-ing* | | We're getting **the 10.00 flight.**
He isn't coming.
I'm meeting **her at the restaurant.** |

Questions
Look back at the two conversations. Underline all the examples of questions in the present continuous.

Use
We use the present continuous to talk about plans for the future.

Practice

Look at these verbs. What are the *-ing* forms?

swim

leave

look

1 Put these words in the right order to make answers to questions.
1 coffee Mary meeting a I'm for
2 restaurant going a Chinese I'm with friends to some
3 TV and in watching staying
4 special nothing
5 for I'm down going London to day the
6 parents spending my I'm couple days of with a

 2 Listen and check your ideas.

3 What do you think the questions are?

 4 Listen to the complete dialogues. Write the questions down.
1 Which answer in exercise 1 can go with all the questions?
2 **In pairs**. Ask each other the questions.
A *What are you doing after this lesson?*
B *I'm ...*

Speak out

1 Work on your own, and choose three things to do this Saturday, and three things to do on Sunday. Mark them:

M = morning
A = afternoon
E = evening

Saturday	Sunday
clothes shopping	tennis
swimming	exhibition
football match	beach
opera	restaurant
cinema	theatre
your own idea	your own idea

2 **In class.** Go round the class and find someone with a similar plan.

A *What are you doing on Saturday?*
B *In the morning I'm ... , and then I'm ...*

Can you remember ...?
• the most popular weekend time for your class
• how to form the present continuous
• how to spell *-ing* forms

Practice *p.90*

3 **Sit with your partner.** Make detailed plans to do the things together. Think about these things.
• When / Where are you meeting?
• What (film) are you seeing?
• Which (restaurant) are you going to?

4 **In groups.** Present your plans. Ask more questions. Continue until everybody has talked about their plans.

12
TRANSPORT & TRAVEL

In this lesson

- Transport vocabulary
- Using public transport
- Understanding announcements

Vocabulary challenge

1 Look at the photographs and complete the puzzle.

2 What's the public transport system like where you live? Are the sentences below true (✓) or false (✗)?

Taxis
1 Taxis are cheap.
2 You can always find one when you need one.
3 People often share taxis.

Trains
1 Lots of people travel by train.
2 Trains are usually late.
3 They're comfortable and clean.

Buses
1 There aren't enough buses.
2 There is always somewhere to sit.
3 Buses run late at night.

Other
1 Lots of people use bikes.
2 People often walk to where they want to go.
3 Ferries are an important form of transport.

3 In pairs. Compare your ideas.

How do you say _____ (in English)?

EXPAND your vocabulary

Try to learn words in groups, e.g. train → *station, platform, ticket*.
What groups can you make for *plane* or *bus*?

English in use
Using public transport

1 [○1] Listen and match the dialogues and the pictures.

2 Listen again and complete these sentences.

  1 Could you _____ , please?

    How _____ ?

    Keep the _____ . And _____ a receipt, please?

  2 Is this _____ Glasgow?

    What time does it _____ ?

  3 What's _____ to get there?

  4 Sorry, _____ did you say?

  5 A _____ to London, please.

3 Look at Tapescript 12.1 on *p.108*. Write down four words from each dialogue. Then close your books and practise the dialogues from memory.

Useful questions

Look at these questions. Which can you ask during a journey?

1 What's the best way to get there?
2 How much is that?
3 Is the flight direct?
4 Do I need to change?
5 How far is it?
6 How long is the journey?

7 Is it better to fly or go by train?
8 Where does the bus leave from?
9 What time do we get there?
10 Could you stop here, please?
11 Is this the bus for London?
12 How often do the buses go to the city centre?

Practice

1 Match the **Useful questions** to these answers.

  a ☐ No, you have to change in Singapore.
  b ☐ Two and a half hours.
  c [1] Probably by taxi.
  d ☐ It depends – flying's much faster.
  e ☐ Yes, sure.
  f ☐ No, it's direct.
  g ☐ £27.50.
  h ☐ About 50 miles.
  i ☐ The central bus station.
  j ☐ No, you want the blue one over there.
  k ☐ Just after 11.00.
  l ☐ Every ten minutes or so.

What's the difference between *How long ...? and How far ...?*
Write a question with each.

2 Listen and check your ideas.

3 In pairs. Practise the dialogues.

 4 Against the clock `2 minutes` Put these words in order to make questions.

1 Which   is London from the train platform leaving to ?
2 How   London is train from the late ?
3 Which   is gate the at flight to boarding Newcastle ?
4 Where   flights British Airways leave do from ?
5 When   it arrive does ?

 5 Now listen to these announcements. Can you complete the answers to the questions in exercise 4?

1 The train to London Paddington is leaving from platform _____ , not platform _____ .
2 The train from London King's Cross is _____ minutes late, and is now arriving at 17.15 .
3 Flight BA1462 to Newcastle is now boarding at gate _____ .
4 All British Airways flights leave from terminal _____ .
5 The flight takes 55 minutes, and arrives at _____ local time.

Can you remember ...?

- six forms of transport
- five useful transport questions
- the difference between *how long* and *how far*

Practice p.91

Speak out

1 Think of three or four cities in your country or a country you know. How can you travel between them? Which is the best way? Think about these things.

- how long?
  - how much?
  - how often?
    → **the best way?**

2 In groups. Discuss your ideas.

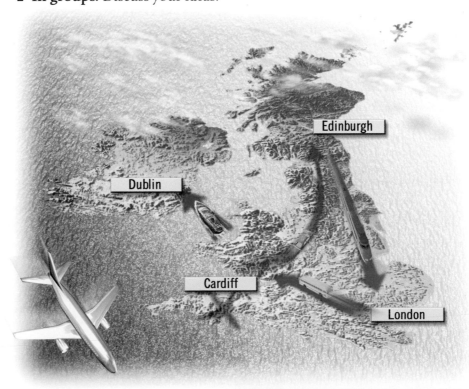

13
HERE & NOW

In this lesson

- Present continuous to talk about now
- Present continuous and present simple

What do you know?

1 In pairs. Read the e-mail below from Vladimir to a friend in Liechtenstein. How many mistakes can you find?

12+ excellent   8–11 good   5–7 not bad   1–4 try again

			13.24
From:	Vladimir	**To:**	Barbara
Subject:	How's the dog?		

Message: Hi! Thanks four the e-mail. I sit on the computa room of Hopeman College. We can book the PCs hear to send e-mails. Its lunchtime, so I have a few minuets …

At the moment were working hard for our English examm – it's dificult. I still working for Pizza Rapide as a water, but I'm pretty sick off it. Spiros and I am look for other works.

How's your dog?

2 In groups. Compare your ideas. How many mistakes have you got now?

3 Share your ideas in class.

Grammar
Present continuous

1 Read what these people are saying on their mobile phones. Match their words to the pictures.

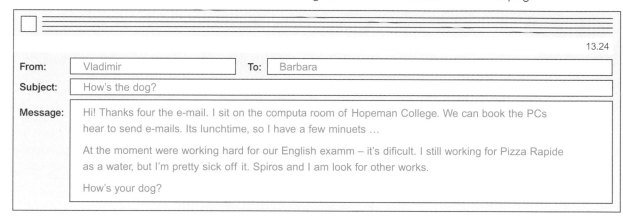

1 You won't believe it. I've got a flat tyre, and it's snowing.

2 I'm sitting in the library … yeah, doing my homework.

3 The view's great – I'm taking loads of photos.

4 We're on our way home now. We've just missed the 5.22 so we're waiting for the next one.

2 Underline all the examples of the present continuous. Do they refer to *now* or *the future*?

Present continuous for now

Form

to be		verb -ing

Look back at *p.35* in lesson 11.

Use

We can use the present continuous to talk about what we're doing now or these days. It's used a lot for talking on mobile phones.

I'm going into the supermarket now. (said on a mobile phone)
I'm having driving lessons at the moment. (talking about these days)

Compare it with the present simple.

I go to the supermarket every day.
I usually have a driving lesson on Thursdays.

Practice

 1 Listen to these three messages on answering machines (don't fill in the spaces).

....

1 *You have one message. Please wait.*

Hi, it's me. I'm on the train. We _____ just _____ the station, and it _____ still _____ . The train's really busy tonight, but at least it's not late, so I should be home soon. I _____ _____ a burger right now, so don't worry about dinner. _____ you.

....

2 *You have no old messages and one new message.*

Hi, it's Michael. I _____ _____ a couple of beers in the pub with John, so I'll _____ home a little late. _____ the dinner warm! Bye.

....

3 *You have one new message.*

Hi, just me. We're on our way back now. Mary wants to pop into the supermarket first. Just what I need ... my feet _____ _____ me. Can you _____ in a pizza? Thanks. Bye.

....

2 In pairs. What can you remember? Try to fill in the missing verbs.

3 Now listen again and check. Which verbs are in the present continuous?

4 Choose the correct form.

1 **I usually get / I'm usually getting** lots of e-mails.
2 **I'm walking / I walk** the dog. I'll be home soon.
3 I'm in the bank. **I'm cashing / I cash** some cheques.
4 On weekdays **we get up / we're getting up** at 7.00.
5 Postmen **do / are doing** a lot of walking.
6 A Where's Jack?
   B **He's fixing / He fixes** the light.

5 Write your own e-mail. Use these cartoons and prompts. Remember to use the present continuous.

- say where you are and what you are doing
- talk about the weather
- discuss your present situation and say what you are doing to change things
- ask a question

Speak out

1 square HEADS

TAILS 3 squares

In pairs. Play this board game. Toss a coin to move. For every picture you land on, say:

• What's happening in the picture

• Why

Listen to each other. If someone makes a mistake, they move back one square. Check with your teacher if necessary.

Can you remember ...?

• the difference between *What do you do?* and *What are you doing?*

• what the three telephone callers are doing

Practice p.92

14
CALLS & MESSAGES

In this lesson

- How you keep in touch
- Contact details
- Taking and leaving phone messages
- Saying phone numbers

Use these words and expressions to help you:

now and again = sometimes
hardly ever = not very often
(quite) often

Speak for yourself

1 ⏱ **Against the clock** 5 minutes How do you communicate?
Put an ✗ on each line and write sentences about yourself.

I write letters now and again.

I write lots of letters.	_____ ✗ _____	I never write letters.
I send e-mails every day.	_____	I never send e-mails.
I use a mobile all the time.	_____	I can't stand mobiles.
I use the phone a lot.	_____	I don't often use the phone.
I meet up with my friends most days.	_____	I hardly ever see my friends.

2 **In groups.** Compare your ideas. Are you similar or different?

Vocabulary

Contact details

1 Match the words with the parts of the business card.

address	☐	telephone number	☐
company name	1	fax number	☐
zip code (GB *postcode*)	☐	job title	☐
e-mail address	☐		
web site	☐		
area code	☐		

What does _____ mean?

[1]HOLDER ENTERPRISES

Howard Skyring
[2]IT Consultant

[3]20344 Mack Avenue
Grosse Point
Michigan 48236[4]
[5](313) 278-1351[6]

(313) 278-[7]1355 (fax)
skyring@holder.com[8]
www.holderent.com[9]

> Some business numbers have extension numbers:
> *Extension 783*

> *44* is usually *double four*, but you can say *four four*.
> *0* is usually *oh*, but people also say *zero*.

2 **In pairs. A** look at *p.105* and **B** look at *p.106*. Find the missing information on your business cards by asking questions.
What's the address / zip code / fax number?

3 How many phone numbers do you have? Tell your partner what they are.
My home number is …
My office / work number is …

English in use
Taking and leaving messages

Michael

Julia

1 Listen to this telephone call and complete the message.

> _____ phoned. Can you call him back on _____ before _____ tonight or _____ tomorrow morning? It's about _____ .

2 Turn to *p.108*. Listen again and read Tapescript 14.1. Is there anything you don't understand?

Useful language

What can you remember? Fill in the missing words.

caller

> _____ Julia?

receiver

> Yes, _____ .

> It's Michael _____ .
> Is Robert _____ ?

> No, _____ .
> Can I _____ a message?

> Yes, _____ . It's _____ the meeting.
> Can he _____ back before 9.00?

> Just let _____ a pen.
> What number can he _____ on?

Practice

1 **Against the clock** `3 minutes` **In pairs.** This phone conversation has 12 mistakes. Can you find them and correct them?

Deirdre	~~Yes?~~ *Hello?*
Jim	Hello, is this Deirdre?
Deirdre	Yes, talking.
Jim	I am Jim. Is George here?
Deirdre	No, I'm sorry. He's at the library. Can I write a message?
Jim	Yes, please. It's of our meeting tomorrow. Can he phone to me back before 7.00 this evening? I'm going out then.
Deirdre	OK, just let me take a pen. Right ... before 7.00. What number can he give you on?
Jim	334 6885.
Deirdre	That's 334 6885. Fine.
Jim	Great. Thanks, Deirdre. Hello.
Deirdre	OK. Hello.

2 Listen and check your ideas.

3 **In pairs.** Read the message.
  1 Write the telephone dialogue to fit.
  2 Practise your dialogue.

4 **In groups.** Perform your dialogues for one another.

> Rachel phoned. Can you call her back on 01688 888777 before 10.00 tonight? It's about the car.

Speak out

1 **In pairs.** Look at the roles below. Take one each.

2 Sit back to back. Practise your telephone conversation. When you have finished, check that the message is correct.

3 **In new pairs.** Change roles and have the conversation again. This time, close your books.

If you have problems understanding people on the phone, say:
Could you say that again, please?
Could you speak a bit more slowly, please?

Can you remember ...?
- six things that appear on a business card
- the difference between a *zip code* and a *postcode*
- how to introduce yourself on the phone

`Practice p.93`

15
UPS & DOWNS

In this lesson

- Different ways of saying *How are you?*
- Feelings vocabulary
- Giving advice

Listening challenge

1 🔲 1 Listen to these people meeting their friends. How does each person start the conversation?

1 _____ ?
2 _____ ?
3 _____ ?
4 _____ ?
5 _____ ?

2 🔲 2 Now listen to the answers. How does each of the friends feel?

😊 5   4   3   2   1 😞

3 **In pairs.** Look at Tapescript 15.2 on *p.108* and practise the dialogues. Show how you are feeling by *how* you answer.

4 Walk around and 'meet' your classmates. How is everyone?

Vocabulary

Feelings

1 **Against the clock** 3 minutes **In pairs.** Put these words in the right column. Use a dictionary to help you.

worried nervous bored
fed up excited tired relaxed
stressed happy angry
upset

feeling good 😊	feeling bad 😞
	worried

How do you say _____ (in English)?

2 Can you add any other words to describe feelings?

3 Complete these sentences with words from the chart. There can be more than one answer.

1 I'm really _____ about my exam.
2 I'm going on holiday tomorrow – I feel very _____ about it.
3 I'm so _____ . My boyfriend's late, I'm cold, I've got no umbrella, and now it's raining!
4 I'm _____ . I'm going to bed.
5 The film was three hours long – I was so _____ !
6 My mum's feeling really _____ , her cat died at the weekend.

 4 Listen. How do these sounds make you feel?

English in use
Giving advice

1 Look at the people in the pictures. How do you think they are feeling?

You can say *I'm nervous*, *I feel nervous*, or *I'm feeling nervous* – there's no difference.

Can you remember two other ways to say *What's the problem?*

2 Now listen to the conversations and match them to the pictures.
1 Do they use the same words as you did to describe their feelings?
2 Why are they feeling that way?

3 Listen to conversation 3 again. This time the friend gives some advice. What does he say? Complete his words.

You _____ _____ to your boss about how you feel, and

you _____ _____ so many hours. You've got a life to live!

1 What words do we use before a verb when we want to give someone advice?

+ _____

– _____

2 Write your own examples, one positive (+) and one negative (–).

When you're tired you _____ .

When you're ill you _____ .

3 Compare your ideas with a partner.

4 **In pairs.** Look at this conversation. What advice would you give?

A You don't look very happy. What's the matter?

B Oh, I've got an exam today and I'm so nervous. I really don't feel very well.

5 Practise the conversation with your piece of advice.

6 Now listen and compare your advice with the advice on the recording. Whose is better?

Speak out

1 Tick (✓) the statements that are true for you.

How do you feel?

I feel very nervous before exams. ☐

I spend a long time deciding what clothes to wear. ☐

I often can't sleep. ☐

I hate going to the dentist. ☐

I can never forget about work. ☐

I often work at the weekend. ☐

I get a lot of headaches. ☐

I never have enough money. ☐

I don't have enough time for my family. ☐

I can't give up smoking. ☐

I eat too much chocolate. ☐

I never get a holiday. ☐

Add a problem of your own if you like:

_____

Can you remember ...?

- three other ways of saying *How are you?*
- eight adjectives to describe feelings
- how to give advice

Practice p.94

2 **In pairs.** Find out more about each other's problems and try to give advice.

16 STARTERS & DESSERTS

In this lesson

- Food and cooking vocabulary
- Understanding menus
- Countable and uncountable nouns

Speak for yourself

1 When do you eat or drink these things? Complete the spidergram.

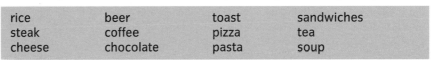

rice	beer	toast	sandwiches
steak	coffee	pizza	tea
cheese	chocolate	pasta	soup

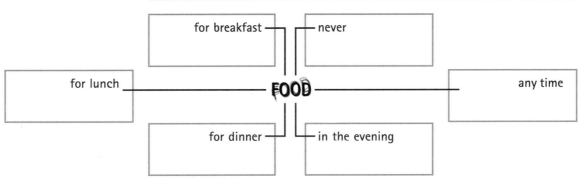

2 Add one more thing to each box. Compare your ideas.

Vocabulary
Food and menus

1 Look at this menu. Which dishes are vegetarian?

grilled salmon with steamed courgettes	**pasta** with tomato and fresh basil sauce	**baked potato** with
fried haddock and chips	**chicken and peppers** with fried or boiled rice	• cheese
roast beef with roast potatoes		• tuna mayonnaise
		• baked beans
		• chilli con carne

2 Look at the menu again and complete the table.

adjectives	verb	food
_ba_ k _ed_	to bake	potato
gr_____	_____	_____
s_____	_____	_____
_____t	_____	_____
f_____d	_____	_____
___i_____	_____	_____

If you know ways of cooking, you'll understand menus more easily. Think about potatoes. How do *you* like them?

3 Try to think of one other food that goes with each verb.

4 How do we make the adjective from the verb? Which adjective is different?

5 **In groups.** Find the words that sound the same in **A** and **B** and add another of your own. Practise pronouncing them.

How do you pronounce _____ ?

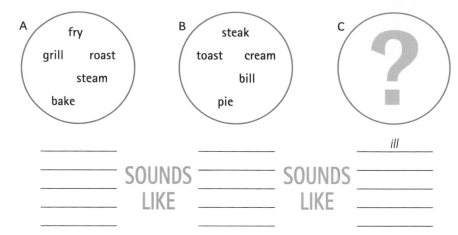

A
fry
grill   roast
steam
bake

B
steak
toast   cream
bill
pie

C
?

_____
_____ SOUNDS _____ SOUNDS _____
_____ LIKE _____ LIKE _____
_____

ill
_____

6 **In pairs.** Write sentences about yourself with adjectives from exercise 2. Read them to your partner.
I like grilled fish.
I really hate boiled potatoes.

Grammar
Countable and uncountable nouns

1 Think of your fridge. Make a list of everything in it. Use these headings.

dairy products	
drinks	
fruit / vegetables	
meat / fish	
other	

Countable	Uncountable
There are **some** ...	There's **some** ...
There are **no** ...	There's **no** ...
Are there **any** ...?	Is there **any** ...?
How many ...?	How much ...?

2 Write some sentences to describe what's in your fridge. Use the phrases in the box above.
There are some eggs in my fridge, but there's no butter.

Practice

1 Correct the mistakes in these sentences.

    1 Have you got any brown breads?

    2 Do you want some spaghettis?

    3 There's no apples.

    4 How many coffee shall I buy?

    5 How much sandwiches are there for lunch?

    6 Can you buy some fruits?

2 **Against the clock** `3 minutes` Make a typical shopping list for people in your country. Include about ten items.

milk
bread
eggs

3 **In pairs.** Compare your ideas. Do you think that the list is different for different countries? If so, how?

EXPAND your vocabulary

If words have an 'opposite', learn the opposite too.
expensive / cheap, open / closed.

What are the 'opposites' of these words?

delicious

red wine

black coffee

sparkling mineral water

strong coffee

Can you remember ...?

• three vegetarian dishes

• five cooking verbs

• the difference between *how much* and *how many*

`Practice p.94`

Speak out

1 Think of a dish you like eating. Prepare to describe it – use these questions to help you.

• What's it called?

• What's in it?

• Is it hot or cold?

• Is it a summer or winter dish?

• Do you eat it on special occasions? When / Where?

2 **In groups.** Describe your dishes. Which would you most like to try? Why?

17
CAFÉS & RESTAURANTS

In this lesson
- Understanding restaurant guides
- Booking a table
- Describing restaurants

Speak for yourself

1 What do you do when you don't want to cook?
Which pictures are like you?

2 **In pairs.** Think about these questions and tell your partner your ideas.
- How often do you eat out?
- What time of day do you eat out?
- Why do you eat out?
- Where do you like eating?
- What type of food do they serve?
- Who do you go with?
- How much do you usually spend?

English in use
Understanding restaurant guides

1 **In pairs.** Look at these headings from an Edinburgh restaurant guide. Can you think of a typical dish or type of food for each kind of restaurant?

*How do you say
_____ (in English)?*

THE BEST FAR-EASTERN RESTAURANTS

THE BEST RESTAURANTS FOR BURGERS AND STEAKS

THE BEST COFFEE SHOPS

THE BEST VEGETARIAN RESTAURANTS

THE BEST CHINESE RESTAURANTS

THE BEST ITALIAN RESTAURANTS

2 Read these descriptions of restaurants and match them with the headings on *p.52*. Underline the words that tell you.

3 One restaurant doesn't have a heading. Which one? What do you think the heading should be?

PHENECIA 662 4493, 55–57 Nicholson St, on corner nr Edin Univ. Yellow Spanish/N African eaterie with couscous, lots of grilled meats and wide vegn choice. Poss to eat v cheaply at lunchtime – some people just pop in for hummus and salad. Lunch Mon–Sat, LO 11pm daily (10pm Sun). **INX**.

CAFÉ FLORENTIN 225 6267, 8 St Giles Street, uptown café with downtown décor, this place combines a range of croissants and wicked tarts with a blast of caffeine, for lawyers and students alike. Open 7.00am to 11pm daily (2am Fri–Sat). **CHP**.

THE ROCK 555 2225, Commercial St. Where to go for lunch or dinner when all you want is a steak/burger and chips (there are other options). Best in town. **MED**.

CAPRICE 554 1279, 325–331 Leith Walk. Old-style – hasn't changed much since the '70s. Pizzas baked to order in a wood-burning oven, kitsch décor but kids love it. It gets busy with families at peak times. Lunch Mon–Sat, LO 11pm Mon–Thu, 11.30pm Fri–Sat, 10pm Sun. **INX**.

ORIENTAL DINING CENTRE 221 1288 8 Morrison St. opp cinema complex. A restaurant and a late-night dim sum and noodle bar. Noodles 5.30pm – 2.30 am Mon–Sat. Restaurant 12 noon–11.30pm daily. **INX**.

ISABEL'S 662 4014, 83 Clerk St. V small café selling vegn standards. No smk. Mon–Sat 11.30am–6.30pm. **CHP**.

DARUMA-YA 554 7660, 82 Commercial St. Japanese dining is often expensive, but at last one that is affordable. Bargain set meals. Lunch Tue–Sat, LO 10.30pm Mon–Sat. Cl Sun. **MED**.

CHP = cheap = less than £12 a head
INX = inexpensive = £12–20 a head
MED = medium = £20–30 a head

Abbreviations are often used in guides.
What do you think the abbreviation for *expensive* is?

4 Find the abbreviations for these words in the restaurant descriptions.

| smoking | near | vegetarian | very |
| possible | Thursday | last orders | closed |

5 **Against the clock** 3 minutes Answer these questions.
1 Where can you go for an early morning cappuccino?
2 What's the phone number of Isabel's?
3 When are last orders at Daruma-Ya?
4 When can you *not* have lunch at Caprice?
5 Where can you eat noodles?
6 Which restaurant has cheap meals?
7 What does *£20 a head* mean?
8 How much is a meal for two at the Rock?

6 **In pairs.** Write three questions of your own and test another pair.

Booking a table

1 Listen to this conversation and complete the gaps.

Waiter	Hello, Caprice.
Customer	Hello, I'd like to _____ a table, please.
Waiter	Certainly, when _____ ?
Customer	This evening, at about 8.30.
Waiter	_____ people?
Customer	Six.
Waiter	Right, let's have a look. Yes, that's fine. And the _____ ?
Customer	Lambeth, _____ L–A–M–B–E–T–H.
Waiter	Thanks, and could I just _____ ?
Customer	Yes, _____ 554 2888.
Waiter	Great. See you at 8.30, Mr Lambeth.

2 Check your ideas in Tapescript 17.1 on *p.109*.

3 **In pairs.** Look at the restaurant guide again. Choose a restaurant and make a dialogue to book a table there.

Can you remember ...?
- three headings from the restaurant guide
- what *nr*, *vegn*, and *Mon* mean?
- three questions you're asked when you book a table

Practice p.96

Speak out

1 Choose a restaurant you like going to and write a short description of it. Use the vocabulary in this lesson to help you.

2 When you've finished, memorize your description.

3 **In groups.** Describe your restaurants. When you're listening to each other, make sure you find out these things.
- where it is
- what it looks like
- what kind of food it serves
- how expensive it is
- opening times

18 SATURDAY & SUNDAY

In this lesson

- Past simple irregular and regular
- Pronunciation of *-ed*
- Talking about your weekend

What do you know?

1 Look at the dialogue. What is wrong with the verbs in **blue**? Correct them.

A How was your weekend?

B Great! I have a fantastic time. On Saturday morning I play tennis, then I go to the cinema with Angela in the evening.

A What do you see?

B *Point Blank*. I think it is great. We meet Rachel in the pub afterwards. What about yours?

A Not bad. Alison comes around. I make dinner for her. She cooks for me last week.

2 **Against the clock** 3 minutes **In pairs.** Which verbs in exercise 1 are **irregular**? Make a list and add any others you know.

3 Can you complete this rule for **regular** verbs?

In the past simple all regular verbs end in the letters _____ .

Grammar

Past simple

1 [CD 1] Listen to a conversation between Bruce and Vic about the weekend, and read the Tapescript on *p.109*. (Circle) all the irregular verbs. How many are from your list? Are there any new ones?

2 Now just listen. Stop the recording when you hear a negative or a question, and write it down. There are five questions and three negatives.

3 What can you remember? Are these sentences true (✓) or false (✗)?

1 Vic saw a film.
2 He loved it.
3 His girlfriend, Sarah, thought it was good, too.
4 They went dancing.
5 He gave Alison a birthday present.
6 Vic phoned Bruce.
7 Bruce had dinner with Karen.
8 She cooked.
9 They both enjoyed the dinner.

Which verb has two past forms? Can you find examples in Tapescript 18.1 on *p.109*?

negative	I he / she / it we you they	✛	didn't	✛	go ... see ... want ...	

infinitive

question	Did	✛	I he / she / it we you they	✛	go ...? see ...? want ...?	⇨	Yes, _____ did. No, _____ didn't.

Practice

1 In pairs, A and B. Play a game of 'Grammar Tennis'.

A Say an irregular verb in the infinitive.

B Say the past simple and score a point. Say another irregular verb in the infinitive.

A Say the past simple and score a point.

... and so on. Who wins?

Remember how to score tennis:	
15–0	*15 love*
15–15	*15 all*
30–30	*30 all*
40–40	*deuce*
40–50, etc	*advantage*

2 In groups of four. Pair **A** take Part 1 of the dialogue between Karen and Sarah. Pair **B** take Part 2.

1 Complete their conversation with the missing past simple verbs.

2 Swap conversations and check each other's work.

Part 1

Karen	Hi there, Sarah.
Sarah	Oh, hi. How ¹w_____ your weekend? How ²w_____ the romantic dinner with Bruce?
Karen	It ³w____'t a great success. I ⁴w_____ round to his place, and he ⁵m_____ dinner for me, but it ⁶w_____ horrible. And then we ⁷h_____ a row. In the end I ⁸l_____ at about 9.30.
Sarah	Oh dear.
Karen	Yeah, well. What about you? What ⁹d_____ you ¹⁰d____?

Part 2

Sarah	I ¹¹w_____ to the pictures with Vic. We ¹²s_____ a film called *Go*. I don't recommend it! Vic really ¹³l_____ it, but I ¹⁴t_____ it ¹⁵w_____ terrible.
Karen	¹⁶D_____ you ¹⁷s_____ Alison?
Sarah	Yeah, we ¹⁸m_____ her in the pub, and she ¹⁹g_____ Vic a CD for his birthday, so he ²⁰w_____ very pleased! Pity you ²¹w_____'t there ...
Karen	You can say that again ...

3 Listen and check your ideas.

4 Listen to these three regular verbs. How do you pronounce *-ed*? Repeat the verbs.

1	2	3
opened	finished	started

How do you pronounce _____ ?

We can use the past simple with *last* and *ago*.

last week / *last* month

five minutes **ago** / *two days* **ago**

Add another example of each.

last _____   _____ ago

5 Say these verbs and put them into the three groups.

stopped	decided	needed	wanted
worked	showed	lived	travelled

6 Complete these sentences with *last* ... or ... *ago*.

I went to the dentist a month ago.

1   I went to the dentist ...
2   I went clothes shopping ...
3   I went out for dinner ...
4   I started learning English ...
5   There was an election in my country ...
6   I bought a new CD ...

Speak out

1 **Against the clock** `2 x 2 minutes` **In pairs.** Ask each other about the weekend again and again and again ...
Take notes as you listen. Who can think of the most answers? Remember to count.

Vary your questions:

And?

What else?

Is that all?

A   *What did you do at the weekend?*
B   *I went for a walk. (1)*
A   *And?*
B   *I went to the theatre. (2)*
A   *What else?*
B   *I brushed my teeth. (3)*

Can you remember ...?

• the past simple of ten irregular verbs

• how to pronounce *wanted*, *opened*, and *worked*

• how to use *last* and *ago*

`Practice p.96`

2 Choose things your partner did which interest you. Ask as many questions as you can about them.

You said you went to the theatre.

When did you go?

What did you see?

Did you like it?

Who did you go with?

Speak for yourself

1 Label this world map.

South America	Europe	Central America
the Far East	Australasia	Asia
the Middle East	Africa	North America
south-east Asia		

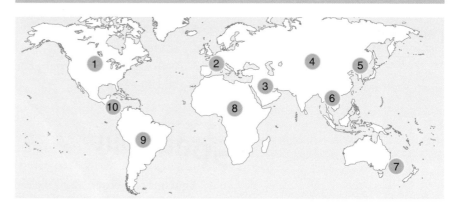

2 In groups. Can you think of one country in each region? Make a list of the countries on the board.

South America   *Venezuela*

3 Which regions or countries would you like to go to? Why?

One day, I'd like to go to _____ because ...

EXPAND your vocabulary

What languages are spoken in the countries you have listed?
What do you call a person who lives there?

Brazil – Portuguese – a Brazilian

We say *the* with plural countries:

***the** United States (of America)*

***the** Philippines*

***the** Netherlands*

We also say ***the** UK*.

Vocabulary
Describing places

How do you pronounce _____?

1 What are these adjectives? There are some letters to help you.

lance   cl_ _ _ = *clean*   tho   h_ _

abefutilu   bea_ _ _ _ _ _   formaboctel   comf_ _ _ _ _ _ _

drocwed   cro_ _ _ _   sinoy   no_ _ _

depullot   pol_ _ _ _ _   nusny   su_ _ _

nereg   gr_ _ _   pexsineve   exp_ _ _ _ _ _

yiturots   to_ _ _ _ _y   talf   fl_ _

2 Look at exercise 1 and find the opposites of these adjectives.

ugly	cheap	uncomfortable	cold
quiet (x2)	cloudy	mountainous	

3 For each adjective in exercise 1 think of something it can describe.

clean   *streets*

beautiful   *countryside*

4 Look at these photos of Lucy's holiday. Where do you think she went?

5 🔘1 Listen to Lucy talking about her holiday. Tick (✓) the adjectives she uses from exercise 1. What do they describe?

Grammar

Comparatives

1 🔘2 Listen to what Lucy says about New Zealand and complete these sentences.

New Zealand was much _____ than Australia. The countryside is a lot _____ and _____ . Unfortunately it's a lot _____ , too, but we thought it was _____ .

Comparatives

Follow the flow chart with *polluted, cloudy, green, hot,* and *crowded*. What are the comparatives?

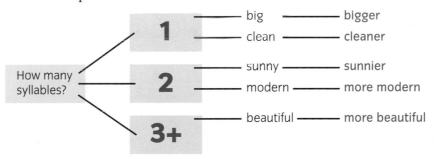

When we want to know about something, we can ask:

Present
What is / are _____ like?

Past
What was / were _____ like?

2 Can you remember these two questions Jan asks about Australia? Check in Tapescript 19.1 on *p.109.*

Jan	_____ ?
Lucy	Absolutely fantastic.

Jan	_____ ?
Lucy	Sunny every day!

Practice

1 Make questions about a holiday, and match them to the answers.

1	What	flight	like ?
2	What	hotel	like ?
3		food	?
4		beaches	?
5		people	?

☐ Really comfortable. The bed was enormous.

☐ Very tasty. Lots of fresh fruit, too.

☐ Very friendly and helpful.

☐ Clean, quiet, and beautiful, and the sea was warm!

1️⃣ It was fine, only two hours.

2 **In pairs.** Ask and answer the questions. This time give negative answers.

A *What was the flight like?*

B *Terrible. It was ten hours, and the films were awful.*

3 Order the words in these sentences comparing different parts of the world, and punctuate them.

1 worse in Britain weather than in is Spain the

2 the the is than Atlantic Pacific larger

3 more you or interesting think is which Tokyo Seoul do ?

4 Town more is expensive in York than Cape shopping New in

5 Belgium than in is Greece in it sunnier

Three comparatives are irregular:

good – *better*

bad – *worse*

far – *further*

Speak out

1 **In pairs.** Make a dictionary of adjectives to describe places. Write these letters on a piece of paper.

a	m
b	n
c	p
e	q
f	s
g	t
h	w

2 Close your books and try to write adjectives for each letter.

3 Think of two countries or cities that you know.

1 In pairs, A and B.

A Compare the places using as many adjectives as you can.

B Listen and tick (✔) the adjectives when you hear them.

2 Change roles.

Can you remember ...?

• six regions of the world

• three words which mean *very good*

• three irregular comparatives

Practice p.98

20
TICKETS & FLIGHTS

In this lesson
- Airport and in-flight vocabulary
- Understanding travel adverts
- Booking a flight

Vocabulary challenge

1 Last month Jonty went on holiday. Look at the words in **blue**. What do they mean? Use a dictionary or ask if you don't know.

He went through passport control.	☐
The plane landed and he got off.	☐
He packed three suitcases.	☐
He checked in and got his boarding pass.	☐
He booked his flight on the Internet.	1
He went to the gate and got on the plane.	☐
He picked up his luggage and walked into the arrival hall.	☐
He watched the in-flight movie and ate two in-flight meals.	☐
The plane took off.	☐
He went to the airport by taxi.	☐
He waited for three hours in the departure lounge.	☐
He went through passport control again.	☐

2 Can you put the things he did in the right order?

3 **In pairs.** Think about the last time you flew. Which of the things in exercise 1 did you do?

*My last trip was to Argentina. I didn't book my flight on the Internet –
I went to a travel agent.*

EXPAND your vocabulary

When you learn nouns, learn verbs that can go with them.

The plane   *took off.*

Cover exercise 1 and try to complete these verbs.

I b_____ my flight.

I p_____ my suitcase.

I w_____ t_____ passport control.

I g_____ o_____ the plane.

I w_____ the in-flight movie.

The plane l_____ .

English in use
Booking by phone

1 Look at this advert for flights. Which place would you go to? Why?
I'd go to Reykjavik. I'd like to see the midnight sun.

 Hot Spanish passion, cool midnight sun

Take advantage of our fantastic last-minute deals to Barcelona and Reykjavik this summer. Book between 8 June and 15 June. Fly from 13 June to 15 August.

Barcelona from £65 rtn

Reykjavik from £150 rtn

Barcelona, a seductive city, rich in culture and full of life. As well as the many sights of the city itself, Barcelona provides easy access to the beautiful beaches of the coast and the spectacular Pyrenees.

Reykjavik, the world's northernmost capital city, has 24-hour sunshine in the summer. Regular concerts, exhibitions and festivals, and the hippest nightclubs in Europe.

Seats can be booked online for a £3 discount at www.fly-away.com, or on 0845 6871111.

Fantastic deals on hotels and car rental also available.

Fares are subject to availability and are inclusive of tax. Conditions apply.

2 Read the advert again. Are these sentences true (✓) or false (✗)?
1 Booking online is more expensive.
2 All flights to Barcelona are £65.
3 Barcelona is a quiet city.
4 It doesn't get dark in Reykjavik in the summer.
5 Reykjavik is a good place for younger people.
6 You can also hire a vehicle if you want.
7 This advert is for online booking only.

3 Complete the answers to these questions. Use the words in the box.

in the morning	myself / me
to book	06
11 Greendykes Road	credit card
Charlbury	possible
OX7 3QQ	

1 **A** How can I help you?
   B I'd like _____ a flight, please.
2 **A** When do you want to travel?
   B 15 July, if _____ .
3 **A** How many people are travelling?
   B Just _____ .
4 **A** What time do you want to travel?
   B Sometime _____ .
5 **A** How would you like to pay?
   B By _____ , please.
6 **A** What's the expiry date?
   B _____ / 05.
7 **A** Could you confirm your address and postcode, please?
   B Yes, it's _____ .

Can you say the dates in the table correctly? Check on *p.05*.

Travel times often use the 24-hour clock.

0900 = *oh nine hundred*

0920 = *oh nine twenty*

1800 = *eighteen hundred*

1845 = *eighteen forty-five*

4 🔊1 Listen to the first part of a conversation booking a ticket by phone. Correct any mistakes in the table.

where?	New York
date / leave?	13 June
date / come back?	1 July
time / leave?	10.50
time / come back?	15.50
price	£90

5 Now listen to the second part. Can you complete the booking form?

Card holder _____

Visa number _____

Expiry date _____

Booking reference _____

Address *Castle Road*

Edinburgh

Postcode _____

6 **In pairs.** Compare your answers. Do you agree?

Speak out

1 **In pairs, A and B.** Act out a telephone booking. Use language from this lesson.

A is the customer who wants to make a booking. Look at the advert on *p.62* and decide:
- where you want to go
- when you want to go / come back
- how many people are travelling
- your credit card number and expiry date
- your address

B is the travel agent. Think about the questions you need to ask:
- where the customer wants to go
- when they want to travel and return
- the number of passengers
- how the customer wants to pay
- the customer's name and address
- any other details, e.g. credit card number

Can you remember ...?
- the sequence of events when you fly
- the attractions of Reykjavik
- three questions a travel agent can ask you

Practice *p.99*

2 Take two minutes to think about the phone call you are going to have.

3 Sit back to back and make your phone call.

21 SINGLES & DOUBLES

In this lesson

- Understanding accommodation guides
- Booking a hotel room

Speak for yourself

1 When you're on holiday, do you normally ...?
- stay in hotels
- book a self-catering apartment
- stay in guest-houses
- go camping
- travel around in a camper van

2 Use these words to write about yourself. Try to give a reason for your choice.

always   usually   sometimes   hardly ever   never

I always stay in a hotel. I don't like making the bed when I'm on holiday.
I never go camping. It's very uncomfortable.

3 **In groups.** Talk about yourself. Where do most people in your group stay when they're on holiday?

Vocabulary
Understanding accommodation guides

1 Look at these symbols from a guide to guest-houses. Match each symbol with a description. Use a dictionary to help you.

- ☐ credit cards accepted
- ☐ packed lunches
- ☐ tea / coffee facilities
- ☐ number of en suite rooms
- ☐ rooms with television
- ☐ central heating
- ☐ pets welcome
- ☐ no smoking

What does _____ mean?

2 In pairs. Cover the descriptions. Point to the symbols and test each other.
 A What does this symbol mean?
 B It means that you can make tea or coffee in your room.

3 Read these advertisements for guest-houses in Ireland. Which do you think is more attractive? Write two or three reasons for your choice.
 I prefer _____ because ...

Gowen House

Victor Road
Cork
00353 21 56641

Comfortable guest-house in the centre of town. Good food and lots of pubs nearby. Large car park. No dogs. Irish music every Friday night.

Waterspring House

nr Cork
00353 21 55123

Warm welcome in lovely old house, beautiful views, good walking. Real fire, books, peace and quiet. 20 mins to centre of Cork.

4 In groups. Tell each other your choice. Do you agree?

English in use
Booking by phone

1 David and Marta are trying to book a room at a hotel in New York. First they phone the Excelsior. Listen and complete the gaps.
 1 They want a room for _____ and _____ .
 2 They want a _____ room with _____ .
 3 The room costs _____ .
 4 The price includes _____

2 Here are some sentences from the dialogue. Reorder the words and decide who says them, David or the receptionist. Listen again to check your ideas.

1 I'd book a like room for this Saturday Friday and to
2 breakfast a free we $225 double with have at
3 phone back I confirm to can later ?

3 🔲2 They now try another hotel. What are the three differences in what this hotel offers?

4 🔲3 Listen to the final conversation. Which room do David and Marta take? Why do you think so?

5 🔲4 **In pairs.** Look at and listen to the useful language for booking a room. Which words are stressed? Practise the sentences.

a double room

a twin room

a single room

Useful language

1 Do you have any rooms free for tomorrow night?
2 I'd like to book a double room for Friday and Saturday.
3 Can I phone back later to confirm?
4 How much is a single / double / twin?
5 Is that with breakfast?
6 I'd like to confirm a booking, please.

Speak out

1 In pairs, A and B.
A You want to book a hotel in Cape Town, South Africa. Look at *p.105*.
B You run a hotel in Cape Town. Look at *p.106*.

Can you remember …?

• four places you can stay on holiday

• five things that a good hotel / guest-house has

• three questions to ask when you book accommodation

Practice p.100

2 A phone **B** and try to book a room. Ask about the facilities the hotel offers. Then change pairs and phone another hotel.

3 A decide which hotel you prefer and phone back to confirm your reservation.

WHEN & WHERE

What do you know?

1 **Against the clock** 1 minute **In pairs.** How many money words do you know? Put them in this chart.

verbs	nouns	adjectives	people
to buy	a bank	rich	a robber
	credit cards		

2 Make a class list of words on the board.

3 **In groups.** Choose **one** of the words. Write a sentence with the word, but leave a space where the word should go.

   I _____ £10 on the lottery last Saturday.

4 Pass your sentence around the class. Can the others guess the missing word?

Grammar
Present perfect and past simple

1 Alex is going to Canada, and wants to know the best way to take money. Listen. What advice does Mark give her?
   - Take traveller's cheques. ☐   • Take credit cards and cash. ☐
   - Take cash. ☐   • Take credit cards. ☐

What's the best way for travellers to carry money in your country?

2 Listen again and tick (✓) these phrases when you hear them.

Have you ever ...?	✓
I've	
I haven't	

3 **In pairs.** Compare your ✓s. Which phrase did you hear twice?

4 Look at Tapescript 22.1 on *p.110*. Write down the words that follow the phrases in exercise 2.

Have you ever ... been to Canada?

All these sentences are in the present perfect tense.

5 Complete this sentence from the listening.

I _____ my wallet on a table in a restaurant ...

What tense is this?

Present perfect

Form

Use

We can use the **present perfect** to **start a conversation** about our past.

Have you ever been to Canada?

We **give details** of the past in the **past simple**.

Yes, just once. I went there two years ago.

Practice

1 Look at this conversation. What are the three forms of the verb?

A **Have you ever won** any money?

B Yes, once.

A How much **did you win**?

B £25. I **won** it on the lottery.

2 Complete the chart of money verbs.

infinitive	past simple	past participle
win	_____	won
borrow	borrowed	_____
lend	_____	lent
_____	found	found
lose	_____	lost
_____	gave	_____
buy	_____	_____

How many times?	
1x	once
2x	twice
3x	three times
4x	four times
2 / 3x	a couple of times
4 / 5x	a few times

3 **In pairs, A and B.** Test each other.

A Say the present perfect question and the past simple question.

B Say the past simple form.

A *Have you ever won? – did you win?*

B *won*

4 In pairs. Look at this questionnaire and interview each other.

Money, Money, Money

1 Have you ever lost your credit card?

2 Have you ever found any money?

3 Have you ever given money to a charity?

4 Have you ever won any money?

5 Have you ever bought something you didn't need?

A Have you ever lost your credit card?
B No, never / Yes, once.
A Really? When was that?
B I lost it in Germany. I was on business ...

Can you remember ...?
*   six money verbs
*   three ways to take money when you travel
*   when to use *Have you ever ...?*

Practice p.101

Speak out

1 Write ten present perfect questions to ask your partner. You can use some of these verbs if you want.

see	study	be	buy	ride	meet
drink	eat	find	fly	read	do

Have you ever been white-water rafting?
*   Write five questions that you think your partner will answer 'No' to.
*   Write five questions that you think your partner will answer 'Yes' to.
*   Don't show each other your questions.

2 **In pairs.** Ask each other your questions. If your partner answers 'yes', ask more questions and find out as much as you can.
*A **Have you ever been** white-water rafting?*
B Yes, once.
A Really? When?
B A couple of years ago.
*A How **was it?***
B Brilliant. We went to ...

3 Did your partner give the answers you expected?

Speak for yourself

1 In pairs. Describe a shop you like. Use these questions to help you.

- Where is it?
- What kind of shop is it?
- What days and times is it open?
- How big is it?
- How often do you go there?
- What do you usually buy?
- Why do you like it?

2 Do you both like the same kind of shop?

Vocabulary

Shops

 1 In pairs. Listen – where is each conversation?
Try to solve the puzzle.

```
1 C           S
   2 C              S H O P
      3 S           S H O P
4 B      S H O P
         5 S                  T
6 P                    E
      7 B        K
8 N              T
```

2 Look at Tapescript 23.1 on *p.110*. Change the words in **bold** and practise the dialogues.

English in use

What's it for?

1 **Against the clock** 5 minutes Make sentences and match them to the pictures. Check with a partner.
They're for cutting paper. picture f

They're for cutting

They're for listening to   messages

music   coffee   They're for locking   It's for paying for

It's for looking up   calls

information   They're for sending

It's for making   postcards   appointments

It's for remembering   new words

paper   It's for making   It's for taking

the door

It's for storing   pictures   It's for taking   the shopping

Scissors are plural and take a plural verb.

These scissors **are** *sharp*.

Can you think of any other words that are always plural?

---

2 **In pairs.** What are the things in the pictures called? Which pair can get the most? Check your answers in class.

3 Test each other.

A *They're for cutting paper.*

B *Scissors.*

EXPAND your vocabulary

Try labelling things, e.g.

This works very well for things in the house. When you know the word, throw the label away.

4 Look at these phrases. Put the words in the right order. Then listen and check.

1 you I ? can help
2 camera you do ? mean a
3 it ? called what's
4 looking for what you ? are
5 in word I the don't English know
6 please you I if wonder could me help
7 it yes that's
8 in called I it's don't what English know

5 Now complete these shop dialogues with the phrases from exercise 4.

1 Assistant   _____ ?
   Customer   Yes, I'm looking for something, but _____ . It's for putting photographs in.
   Assistant   Oh, a photo frame.
   Customer   _____ .

2 Customer   Hello. _____ .
   Assistant   Of course. _____ ?
   Customer   That's the problem – _____ . It's for taking photographs.
   Assistant   _____ ?
   Customer   No, the thing in the camera. _____ ?
   Assistant   Oh, the film.
   Customer   Yes, that's it.

6 Listen and check. Look at Tapescript 23.3 on *p.110* and practise the dialogues.

Speak out

In pairs. Look at the pictures on *p.71* again. Choose one or more things you would like to buy and practise similar dialogues to the ones in exercise 5. Act out your dialogues to another pair.

Can you remember ...?

• six names of shops
• how to ask for things when you don't know the word in English

Practice p.102

24
SUITS & BOOTS

In this lesson

- Clothes vocabulary
- Clothing categories
- Going clothes shopping

Vocabulary challenge

1 **Against the clock** `2 minutes` **In pairs.**
   A Write down as many clothes as you can.
   B Write down as many colours as you can.

2 Compare your lists. How many more words can you add?

3 Think about your most recent weekend away. What clothes did you take?

   I took my black jumper, and a couple of T-shirts, one white, one blue ...

Vocabulary

What to wear

1 Match these clothes and accessories with the pictures.

a jumper	a suit	walking boots	gloves
a briefcase	cargo pants	trainers	a waterproof jacket
a fleece	a backpack	a bag	a cap

2 Find a person in the class for each of the items. Write their name beside the item.
   A *Have you got a waterproof jacket?*
   B *Yes, I have. Have you got a pair of walking boots?*
   A *No, I haven't. Have you?*

Can you think of two other clothes with *suit*?

t_____suit

s_____suit

How do you
pronounce _____?

We can use *pair of* with 'plural clothes'.

I've got some jeans / two pairs of jeans.

Can you think of more plural clothes?

3 Look at this page from an Internet shopping site. Which words would you click if you want the things in exercise 1?

a jumper   *tops*

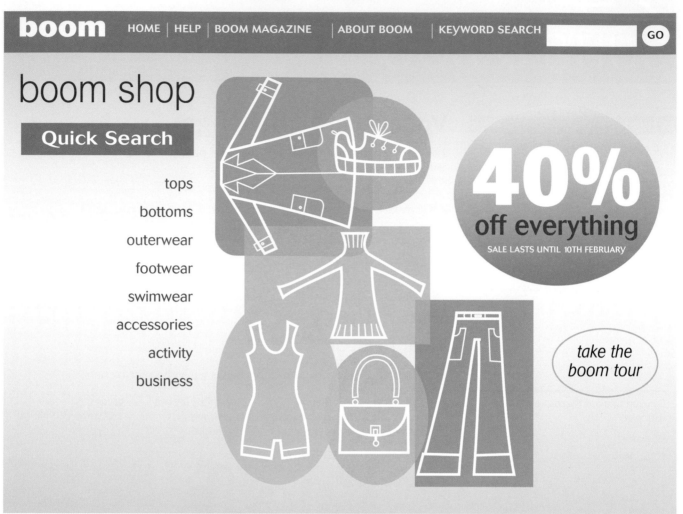

boom   HOME | HELP | BOOM MAGAZINE | ABOUT BOOM | KEYWORD SEARCH [   ] GO

boom shop

Quick Search

tops
bottoms
outerwear
footwear
swimwear
accessories
activity
business

40%
off everything
SALE LASTS UNTIL 10TH FEBRUARY

take the boom tour

4 Listen to these five people. What clothes and accessories are they talking about? Choose from exercise 1.

English in use
Going clothes shopping

1 In a clothes shop, who would say these things – the customer (**C**), the customer's friend (**F**), or a shop assistant (**A**)?

1 It looks great / nice / good. ☐
2 Any good? ☐
3 Just looking, thanks. ☐
4 Are you all right there? ☐
5 Yeah, I'll take this one, please. ☐
6 It doesn't really suit you. ☐
7 Can I help you? ☐
8 Yes, have you got these in a large? ☐
9 What do you think? ☐

What does _____ mean?

2 Complete the dialogues under the pictures with phrases from exercise 1.

1 Assistant *Are you all right there?* Customer _____	2 Assistant _____ Customer _____	3 Customer _____ Friend _____	4 Assistant _____ Customer _____

 3 Listen and check your answers.

4 In pairs. Listen again and practise the dialogues together.

5 Match all the sentences that mean the same thing.

Can I help you? —————— It looks really nice.

What do you think? ———— This one will be fine.

It looks great. ————————— Any good?

I'll take this one, please. ——— I'd like this one, please.

How does it look?

Do you need any help?

Are you all right?

6 Change partners. Close your books and practise the dialogues in exercise 4 again. Try to use as many different phrases as you can.

Speak out

1 Write five questions about clothes and shopping for clothes. Use one or more of the words below in each question.
What do you like wearing in the evenings?

Can you remember …?

* four things you wear when it's cold
* three things you pack for a weekend away
* three things you say in a clothes shop

Practice p.103

where? favourite wear expensive like
work evenings colour how?
sport when? buy
shopping comfortable money what?

2 Answer your own questions on a piece of paper.

3 Ask other students your questions. Whose answers are the most similar to yours?

PRACTICE

01

The alphabet

1 Put these words into alphabetical order, as in a dictionary. Look up any words you don't understand.

1	see	bake	use	run	watch
2	hot	cold	cool	cloudy	windy
3	question	quick	queue	quiet	quite
4	stand	stamp	start	star	stadium
5	green	grey	Greek	great	greedy

Names and spelling

2 Write the complete questions.

A What / first name?   _____

B Anna.

A What / surname?   _____

B Harrap.

A How / spell that?   _____

B H-A-R-R-A-P.

3 Are these first names for men (**M**) or women (**W**)? If you don't know, guess.

Becky	☐	Sean	☐
Liam	☐	Russell	☐
Sharon	☐	Greg	☐
Ruth	☐	Penny	☐
Duncan	☐	Heather	☐

Dates

4 Answer these questions.
1 Which month has the most letters?
2 Which month has the fewest letters?
3 How many months end in -ember?
4 Which month sometimes has 29 days? How often?
5 How many months begin with J?
6 Which month do you like most? Why?
7 When is Christmas Day / Valentine's Day / New Year's Day?
8 What's the date today?
9 What's the date a week tomorrow?
10 What was the date last Friday?

Numbers

5 Match the numbers and the descriptions.

20°	date
30 mph	speed
0191 556 2233	temperature
6758 4521 6666 9988	postcode
30/6/99	bus number
OX7 2PP	credit card number
£4.99	year
1821	telephone number
15A	price

6 Put these words in the right order to make questions.
1 speed in country your limit what's the ?
2 a is ? cappuccino large much how
3 at weather like moment what's ? the the
4 China ? code for what's the
5 ? number flight the what's

7 Now match the questions above with these answers.
☐ $1.50.
☐ VA0198.
☐ Hold on ... it's 00 86.
☐ 120 kph, but a lot of people drive faster.
☐ It's been very hot, over 40° last week.

Form filling

8 Fill in these details for a credit card application.

Your personal details

Mr ☐ Mrs ☐ Miss ☐ Ms ☐ Other title _____

Surname _____

First name(s) _____

Date of birth _____

Your home

House / Flat number _____

Street _____

City _____

Postcode _____

Time at present address

_____ years __ _____ months

Home telephone number (with code) _____ _____

Are you (tick the box)

a home owner ☐   a tenant ☐   living with parents ☐

Your employment

Are you (tick the box)

employed ☐

self-employed ☐

retired ☐

a student ☐

unemployed ☐

Occupation _____

Business telephone number (with code) _____

Additional information

Please include your e-mail address if you have one

_____

02

Countries and nationalities

1 Complete these countries.

1 __pain
2 __apa__
3 _____many
4 _____zil
5 Ire_____
6 S_____den
7 the _____ed St_____
8 Fran____
9 I_____y
10 Ch____a
11 Aus_____l____
12 the N_____lands

2 Now complete the table of nationalities with the countries from exercise 1.

-ish	-an / -ian	-ese	other
Spanish		Japanese	

to be, present and past

3 Complete these questions and find the answers.

1 Where _____ James yesterday?
2 Who _____ that woman over there?
3 _____ John and Alice at school?
4 _____ you from the States?
5 What _____ his job?
6 Where _____ Karen?
7 _____ Sam coming to the cinema?
8 How _____ your parents?
9 _____ you on holiday last week?
10 _____ I late?

☐ She's on holiday.
☐ She's the new personnel manager.
☐ He's an accountant.
☐ No, they're visiting their grandparents.
☐1 He was in London.
☐ Only five minutes.
☐ No, he isn't, he's busy this evening.
☐ They're fine.
☐ No, I was off sick.
☐ No, I'm Canadian.

4 Put the words in the right order to make questions. Then find the answers in the two e-mails on *p.08*.

1 Marzia is from where ?
   A *Where is Marzia from?*
   B *She's from Parma, in Italy.*
2 her what job is ?
   A _____ ?
   B _____
3 like her is pay what ?
   A _____ ?
   B _____
4 was where last Jim year ?
   A _____ ?
   B _____
5 with who he was ?
   A _____ ?
   B _____

6 was what the like weather ?

A _____ ?

B _____

7 what the was like food ?

A _____ ?

B _____

8 before when they were there ?

A _____ ?

B _____

Pronouns

5 Complete these answers.

1 **A** Are the Andes in Africa?

 B No, *they aren't, they're in* South America.

2 **A** Is Nairobi the capital of South Africa?

 B No, _____ , _____ Kenya.

3 **A** Was John Lennon one of the Rolling Stones?

 B No, _____ , _____ Beatles.

4 **A** Was Mozart German?

 B No, _____ , _____ Austrian.

5 **A** Are whales fish?

 B No, _____ , _____ mammals.

6 **A** Were Sally and Andrea in Hungary last week?

 B No, _____ , _____ Poland.

7 **A** I think her name's Stephanie.

 B No, _____ , _____ Elizabeth.

8 **A** You're from the States, aren't you?

 B No, _____ , _____ .

6 Complete the spaces with pronouns.

1 | The weather
  It _____ | was foggy yesterday.

2 | My wife
  _____ | was in hospital last month.

3 | The house
  _____ | is for sale.

4 | John's parents
  _____ | were here yesterday.

5 | Mr Klein
  _____ | is a businessman.

6 | My friends and I
  _____ | are going shopping.

03

Relationships vocabulary

1 Look at the family tree. What relation are these people to Helen?

Mark _____*husband*_____

Michael _____

Holly _____

Maria _____

Jane _____

Stanley _____

Justin _____

Bernie _____

John _____

Janet _____

Harry _____

Sally _____

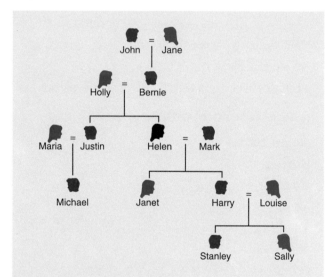

2 Read what Helen says about her family. <u>Underline</u> the mistakes and correct them.

1 I've got <u>two brothers</u>.
  I've got one brother.

2 My grandfather's name is Jack.

  _____

3 I've got three children.

  _____

4 My daughter has two children.

  _____

5 I've got two nephews.

  _____

6 My sister-in-law is called Caroline.

  _____

7 Stanley is my granddaughter.

  _____

8 Harry's sister is called Jane.

  _____

have got / has got

3 Complete these sentences with the correct form of *have got* or *has got*.

1 She ___'s got___ fair hair.
2 They _____ two children.
3 I can't come. I _____ a ticket.
4 A Where's the TV guide?
   B I think Ben _____ it upstairs.
5 Can I borrow a fiver? I _____ any money.
6 I love Edinburgh. It _____ just about everything you need.
7 Mary _____ a toothache.
8 Mr and Mrs Davies _____ a new Mercedes.
9 The bookshop across the road _____ the best selection of books I know.
10 He _____ a car. He can't afford it.

4 Write the questions. Then answer them yourself.

1 any change
   A *Have you got any change?*
   B *Yes, I have / No, I haven't.*
2 any brothers and sisters
   A _____ ?
   B _____
3 a mobile
   A _____ ?
   B _____
4 any plans for the weekend
   A _____ ?
   B _____
5 a light
   A _____ ?
   B _____
6 a big family
   A _____ ?
   B _____

House and home vocabulary

5 Complete the description of a flat with the words in the box.

reading	balcony	living room	bedrooms
building	watching	floor	dining room

We live in a flat in the centre of Bristol. It's in a big Victorian ¹_____ , on the top ²_____ . There's a big ³_____ where we spend most of our time, ⁴_____ TV or ⁵_____ by the fire. There isn't a ⁶_____ – we eat at a table in the kitchen. There are three ⁷_____ , though one of them is very small, and a little ⁸_____ with a view over the park. We haven't got a garden, but that's OK, we don't like gardening anyway!

6 Write these things in the correct room.

soap	dishwasher	coffee table
wardrobe	hi-fi	pillow
towels	pots and pans	toilet paper
duvet	bookcase	washing-up liquid

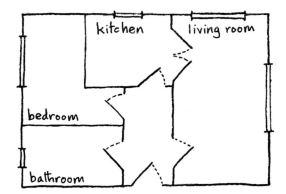

British and American English

1 Put these words in the right column.

favourite	theater	center	colour
favorite	theatre	centre	color

British spelling	US spelling

2 Match the words with the same meaning.

British English	American English
flat	elevator
lift	soda
boot (of a car)	trunk
fizzy drink	highway
motorway	apartment

Read the texts. Where do the people live? There are two texts for each place.

a house in the suburbs ☐ ☐   a flat in the city centre [1] ☐   a house in a small village ☐ ☐

1 It's small, only one bedroom, but that's enough for me. It can be very noisy at night, but it's great being so near cinemas and restaurants.

2 All the houses look the same round here, but they're quite nice, with three bedrooms. We've got a small garden, too.

3 The worst thing is doing the shopping, because there isn't a shop here.

4 It's the best of both worlds – it's easy to get to the city centre, and easy to get out into the country.

5 I'm on the top floor, but there's a lift. The view over the rooftops is great.

6 I don't see my friends as often as I'd like to, but they sometimes come to stay for the weekend, and we go for walks.

Writing

Look at Helen's family tree in exercise 1. Draw one for yourself, and write a description of your own family. Include as many different relations as possible.

04

Daily routines

1 Choose the correct verb.
   1 I **take** / **have** a coffee every morning.
   2 I **go** / **drive** to work by bike.
   3 I **watch** / **look at** TV in the evening.
   4 I **visit** / **go** friends at the weekend.
   5 I **see** / **read** the paper every day.

2 Look at the picture and label the sentences A or B.
   I have a cocktail before dinner.   [A]
   I drive to work – I get there at about 8.30.   ☐
   I play tennis with friends in the afternoon.   ☐
   I don't have a lunch break – just coffee in the office. ☐
   I get home at around 8.00 in the evening.   ☐
   I get up at 6.30 in the morning.   ☐
   I get up at about 10.00.   ☐
   I have breakfast by the pool.   ☐

3 Now put the sentences for the two men in the right order.

A	B
	I get up at 6.30 in the morning.

4 Write down two things you do for each topic.

Work   *I work in a hospital.*
               I start at half past seven every morning.

Work

Free time

Food / Meals

Entertainment

Shopping

Clothes

Holidays

Present simple

5 Complete the sentences with the correct form of these verbs.

live	move	smoke	open
watch	drink	have	change
meet	speak		

1 Simon _speaks_ French, German, and a little Spanish.
2 My mother _____ eight cups of tea a day.
3 The National Museum _____ from Monday to Saturday.
4 They _____ a lot of videos.
5 I _____ toast and marmalade for breakfast. Delicious!

6 The weather in Britain _____ from day to day.
7 Most snakes _____ away if they hear you coming.
8 He _____ a lot of people in his job.
9 My father _____ 20 a day.
10 You _____ in the city, don't you?

6 Make sentences with a negative.

1 Simon speaks French / Russian
Simon speaks French but he doesn't speak Russian.

2 My mother drinks tea / coffee

3 The National Museum opens from Monday to Saturday / Sunday

4 They watch videos / go to the cinema

5 I have toast for breakfast / cereal

7 Now ask questions for these answers.

1 A *What languages does Simon speak?*
  B French, German, and Spanish.
2 A _____ ?
  B Eight cups a day.
3 A _____ ?
  B From Monday to Saturday.
4 A _____ ?
  B No, they watch videos.
5 A _____ ?
  B Toast and marmalade.

every

8 Write six sentences about your life with these phrases.
I listen to the news on the radio every morning.

every morning
every week
every day
every couple of years
every Sunday
every evening

Reading a timetable

9 Look at the airline timetable and answer the questions.

A What time is the first flight from London?

B 06.55.

1 What time does the five past eight morning flight from London arrive in Berlin?

2 What is the flight number of the four o'clock afternoon flight from Berlin?

3 How many morning flights are there from London?

4 What time is the last flight from Berlin?

5 Which flight must you catch if you want to arrive in London before nine in the evening, but cannot leave Berlin until after six?

6 Which days is there a London–Berlin flight at quarter to one?

From London Heathrow to Berlin – Tegel »

Time		Days of week	Flight number
depart	arrive		
06:55	09:45	MTWThF	BA970
08:05	10:50	SaSu	BA972
12:45	15:35	MWF	BA966
16:00	18:40	TThSa	BA964
19:50	22:35	all	BA958

From Berlin – Tegel to London Heathrow »

Time		Days of week	Flight number
depart	arrive		
10:25	11:30	MTWThF	BA971
11:25	12:30	SaSu	BA973
16:00	17:05	MWF	BA967
19:05	20:10	TThSa	BA965
23:30	00:40	all	BA959

05

Present simple

1 Read part of a letter from Jeremy to a friend. Are the sentences true (✓) or false (✗)?

I'm sending a photo of Jill and me on holiday in Greece this year. She's fine and sends her love. She's just got a new teaching job! Do you remember Bill? Well, he teaches at the same school. Jill goes to work with him. Generally she's happy with the job, but she can't stand the head teacher. He pushes his staff a lot, I think. All I know is she's happy to get home. She finishes at 4.00 most days but that's not the end of her day. She studies most evenings too – she's got an exam in May. Hard work!

1 Jill and Jeremy are on holiday. ☑

2 Bill's a teacher. ☑

3 Bill and Jill work together. ☑

4 Jill loves everything about her job. ☑

5 The head teacher makes his staff work hard. ☑

6 Jill always finishes work at the same time. ☑

2 What are these verbs? Which one isn't in the letter above?

1 shupes   p_____

2 sego   g_____

3 shinifes   f_____

4 cheates   t_____

5 chatsew   w_____

6 sidutes   s_____

Writing

Look back at exercises 2 and 3. Choose one of these people and write about their daily routine.

3 Correct the spelling mistakes in these sentences.

1 Mary watchs soap operas to relax.
2 He studys in the evenings after work.
3 Ally gos to work by bus.
4 Jack finishs work before me.
5 Jackie boxs cans of Coke in a factory.
6 Dan pases our house on his way to work.

4 Read the texts about Becky and Ruth on *p.16* and *p.17*. Match these question words with the answers.

What time?	Because there aren't enough chairs and desks.
Where?	Fish, rice, and sweet potato.
Who?	In leaf hut classrooms.
How often?	Nine o'clock.
What?	Once a year.
Why?	A local family.

5 Now write the questions in full.

1 *What time does Becky start work?*
2 _____ ?
3 _____ ?
4 _____ ?
5 _____ ?
6 _____ ?

Adverbs of frequency

6 Rewrite these sentences with the word in (brackets).

1 The bus is early.
(often)
The bus is often early.

2 Janice finishes work early.
(often)
_____

3 I just sit and do nothing.
(sometimes)
_____

4 He watches TV.
(hardly ever)
_____

5 Mark does the washing-up.
(never)
_____

6 What time do you get up?
(usually)
_____

7 We don't eat meat.
(always)
_____

8 They're late.
(often)
_____

Weather

7 Match the words and the symbols.

1 windy *e*   4 cold *a*
2 sunny *f*   5 hot *d*
3 rainy / wet *b* 6 snowy *c*

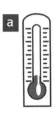

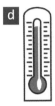

8 What's the weather like where you live? Add an adverb of frequency to these sentences. If possible say *when*.
*It's **sometimes** windy where I live, especially in the summer.*

1 It's windy.
_____

2 It's sunny.
_____

3 It rains.
_____

4 It's cold.
_____

5 It's hot.
_____

6 It snows.
_____

06

Jobs and occupations

1 Complete these jobs with *-or* or *-er*.

solicit____   act____
decorat____   wait____
farm____   plumb____
sail____   translat____
writ____   bank manag____

2 Match the jobs and the places. (Sometimes more than one answer is possible.)

I'm

an au pair.
a businesswoman.
a computer programmer.
a doctor.

a secretary.
a teacher.
a lawyer.
an architect.

I work

in a children's hospital.
in a school near here.
for a multinational company.
for a family in America.
in a computer lab in the university.
in an office in the centre of town.

3 Complete the puzzle with the person who can help with each problem (you can use a dictionary to help you). What's the word down the middle?

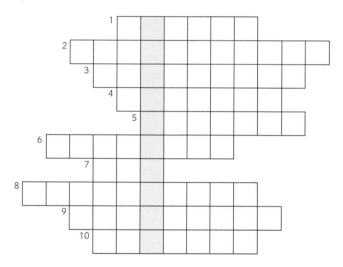

1 Jamie's not well.
2 We need a new light switch.
3 We want to design a new house.
4 We need someone to build it!
5 There's water all over the floor.
6 My car's broken down.
7 My cat's sick.
8 We need someone to look after the kids tonight.
9 The kitchen needs painting.
10 Our son's got an awful toothache.

4 Write out the letters of the alphabet and make your own 'jobs' dictionary.

a   architect, artist, author
b   builder, bank manager
c
d
e
f
g

Job adverts

5 Complete this advert with the words in the box.

experience	salary	skills	motivated
a degree	details	applicants	essential

WORLDWATCH
Environmental charity

We require a fund-raising manager to help us maintain our position in the competitive world of environmental charities.

¹ _____ should have five years'
² _____ in a related field, and
³ _____ in an earth science. Knowledge of fund-raising is ⁴ _____ . Applicants should be ⁵ _____ and have good communication ⁶ _____ .

The ⁷ _____ is in the region of £25K.

For more ⁸ _____ , e-mail h.thomas@worldwatch.org.uk

Reading

Read the text and choose **a** or **b** to complete the sentences.

1 He often works   a) eight hours a day.
                      b) twelve hours a day.

2 His favourite part of the job is   a) the research.
                      b) the teaching.

3 He   a) never works overnight.
       b) occasionally works overnight.

4 He spends most of his time   a) correcting exams.
                      b) working in the laboratory.

5 He likes   a) most things about his job.
                      b) everything about his job.

6 He thinks academics have   a) an easy life.
                      b) a difficult life.

7 He goes on a work trip abroad   a) once a year.
                      b) twice a year.

8 He   a) likes what he does.
       b) doesn't like what he does.

A day in the job of
Graham Rowe, biologist, Exeter University

My working day doesn't usually start very early, maybe around 10.00. My job involves some teaching, but it's mainly research. If I'm teaching, I often give a couple of lectures in the morning, and then I sometimes have students' work to look at in the afternoon, or exams to correct, which can be very time-consuming. Lunch is a sandwich, and I drink constant cups of coffee through the day.

The research is what I really enjoy, and I often stay in the laboratory till 9.00 or 10.00, even overnight once in a while. I've got two post-graduate assistants, and we all work fairly long hours, including weekends. Anyone who thinks that academics have an easy life should come and work with me! The good side of it is that I get to travel for a month in the summer, usually to Kenya or Tanzania.

There isn't much that I don't like about the job – there's sometimes quite a lot of university paperwork, which can be annoying when I want to be in the lab ...

07

Likes and dislikes

1 Read the advert and match the activities to the pictures.

WILD AMERICA
Where the crowds don't go!

Biking, hiking, rafting, horse-riding, canoeing, city sightseeing and more!
For a free brochure, call *Wild America*
01298 344552

2 Tick (✓) the activities you enjoy doing.

3 The advertisement says ... *and more!* Think of three other activities the travel company could offer. Use a dictionary to help you.

4 Look at Mary's Internet favourites. Write five sentences.

She (really) likes
She enjoys   *playing / watching tennis.*
She's interested in

Favourites ▷ **Organize** ▷

new folder
new favourites
Toolbar Favourites
new divider
Wimbledon tennis c
open favourites window
Bicycle links
Delta Airlines
Italy visitors' guide
South America Onlir
Film listings Dublin
MP3 latest hits
Sports results footba
Speak Italian
MusicMusicMusic!
computer sales lapto

5 Compare yourself to Mary. If you don't like the same things as her, say what you like doing.
I don't like playing tennis, but I like watching it.

6 Rewrite the sentences using the verb in (brackets).

1 He goes to the gym every day.
   (like)
   He likes going to the gym.

2 They go to the cinema most weekends.
   (enjoy)
   _____

3 Mary gardens every weekend.
   (love)
   _____

4 John drives whenever he can.
   (love)
   _____

5 We never play computer games.
   (hate)
   _____

6 George spends a lot of time with his children.
   (enjoy)
   _____

7 I never get up early.
   (can't stand)
   _____

8 I think the dentist is OK.
   (don't mind)
   _____

-ing forms

7 What are the *-ing* forms of these verbs?

drive	_____
take	_____
get	_____
hope	_____
watch	_____
cycle	_____
teach	_____
study	_____

08

Entertainment

1 Look at the diagram and the example. How long does it take you to get to these places from your home? Put them in the correct circle and write sentences.
It takes me 20 minutes to get to the cinema by bus.

cinema theatre	museum zoo	café restaurant	art gallery bar

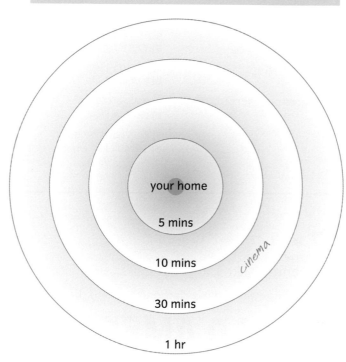

2 How often do you go to the places above?
I go to the cinema about once a month.

3 Tick (✓) the sentences that describe you. Can you add two more?

I always go out at the weekend. ☐
I'm a football fanatic – I go to all my team's games. ☐
I love going to the cinema. ☐
I can only relax when I'm with people. ☐
I like staying in. ☐
I enjoy museums a lot. ☐
I eat out at least once a month. ☐
I really like concerts. ☐
I normally don't go out during the week. ☐
I hate zoos. ☐

_____

_____

4 Think of a friend or relation. Write ten sentences about them like the ones in exercise 3.

1 *My best friend, Arancha, sometimes goes out at the weekend.*

2 *She hates football and never goes to football matches.*

Prepositions

5 Complete the sentences with the correct prepositions.

1 What's _____ at the cinema this week?
2 The bus stops right _____ the theatre.
3 The restaurant's _____ Grindlay Street.
4 We're going out to eat _____ that restaurant _____ Saturday evening.
5 We're taking my parents _____ an art gallery.
6 **A** How are you getting home?
   B _____ taxi, probably.
7 Can you book tickets _____ phone?
8 On Sundays you can get _____ free.

Describing places

6 Complete these sentences from a Vienna travel guide with the words in (brackets).

1 The cinema has an film festival.
(international)
The cinema has an international film festival.
2 This restaurant has a menu.
(friendly / creative)
3 This café has the waiters in town.
(best / old-fashioned)
4 The city park accommodates an zoo.
(beautiful / excellent)
5 The standard hours for museums are 10 a.m–6 p.m. in summer.
(opening / all)
6 Vienna has about 150, most in the city centre.
(art galleries / of them)
7 This wine bar has music – jazz, blues on Fridays.
(live / on Mondays)
8 Club 66 is till 6.00 a.m. on Saturdays and.
(Sundays / open)
9 The theatre is very and is still the home of Austrian.
(glamorous / drama)

09

Places in a city

1 Find nine other places in this word square.

u	p	c	h	i	p	s	h	o	p	o	t	k
u	k	g	w	g	l	r	e	p	b	l	a	p
n	v	b	b	m	w	o	b	k	m	d	z	h
d	v	k	r	s	s	u	i	p	b	j	k	b
e	n	c	i	u	h	n	c	q	u	r	a	o
r	t	h	d	t	o	d	k	l	s	k	j	e
g	b	e	g	c	e	a	p	r	s	e	a	q
r	u	m	e	o	s	b	m	b	t	k	m	h
o	b	i	q	w	h	o	v	u	o	o	f	d
u	b	s	j	t	o	u	a	k	p	a	r	k
n	n	t	x	h	p	t	p	q	x	n	j	z
d	m	s	p	o	s	t	o	f	f	i	c	e
r	t	r	a	i	n	s	t	a	t	i	o	n

2 What are these places? Match them with the definitions.

1 mastidu   s_____
2 cie-krin   i__-_____
3 quesra   s_____
4 lalm   m_____
5 trop   p_____ _

☐ an indoor area for skating
☐ a covered shopping centre
☐ a place for ships, boats, and ferries
☐ an area for games and competitions, e.g football, rugby, athletics, with seats for spectators
☐ an open area with four sides, usually in the centre of a town, often with cafés and shops

---

Reading

Read the text about the Tate Modern art gallery and write questions for the answers.

1 *Where is it?*
   It's on Bankside.
2 7887 8000.
3 It's http://www.tate.org.uk.
4 It's usually free.
5 10.00 in the evening.
6 It's on level 7.

Tate Modern
Bankside   020 7887 8000
London SE1 9TG   http://www.tate.org.uk

Nearest tube ⊖ Southwark, Jubilee Line
Admission: Free
There may be charges for temporary exhibitions and special events.
Opening Hours: Sun – Thurs 10.00–18.00, Fri – Sat 10.00– 22.00
Restaurant: On level 7 to seat 160
Café: On level 2 to seat 240
Auditorium: On level 2 to seat 260

Writing

1 Look at these useful phrases you can use in letters to friends.

Thank you very much for your | e-mail. / postcard. / letter.

It was | great / wonderful | to hear from you.

Sorry I haven't written for so long.

I hope | you're / your family's | well.

Say hello to | Michael / your mother | for me.

Write / E-mail | soon!

2 Now read this letter and <u>underline</u> the phrases.

3 Write a letter to a friend inviting them to come and stay with you.

56 Cherwell Way
Brighton
BN6 9JL
22 November

Dear Cristina,
Thank you very much for your postcard – it was great to hear from you. I hope the children are well.

Have you got any plans for holidays next year? If you ever want to come to London, you can always stay with me. I've got plenty of room! You should stay for at least a few days, there's a lot to do. I live quite near the zoo, which I'm sure the kids would like. There are lots of great restaurants, and you can get to the centre on the underground in about 20 minutes, so we could go to the theatre too. What do you think?

Say hello to David for me, and write soon!
Love,
Kay

British and American English

1 Which word in exercise 2 on *p.87* is American?

2 Match these American places with the British ones.

liquor store	block of flats
rest room	off-licence
drugstore	shop
the subway	car park
gas station	chemist's
apartment building	the underground
parking lot	public toilet
store	petrol station

liquor store — off-licence

Asking for directions

3 Put these words in the right order to make questions.

1 you museum me where could the is please tell ?

2 restaurant is here Chinese a near ? there

3 is the to Italian the ? restaurant this way

4 there's ? you do if a here chemist's know near

4 Match the two parts to make questions. (Sometimes there is more than one possibility.)

Excuse me ...

	this the way to the library?
Is there	the stadium near here?
Could you tell me	if there's a park near here?
Is	for a book shop.
Do you know	a newsagent near here?
I'm looking	where the railway station is, please?
How do I get to	the way to the police station?
	a public convenience near here?
	the shopping centre?

Prepositions

5 Look at the map. Which places are the people talking about?

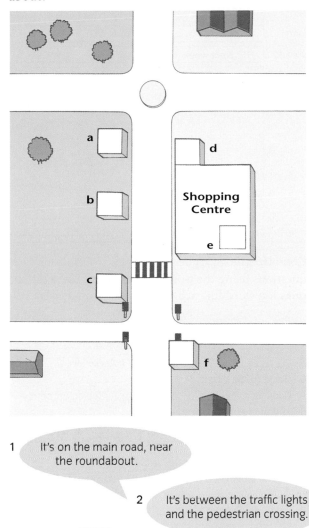

1 It's on the main road, near the roundabout.

2 It's between the traffic lights and the pedestrian crossing.

3 It's in the shopping centre.

4 It's next to the shopping centre.

5 It's opposite the shopping centre.

6 It's on the corner.

Test your spelling lessons 07–09

Can you correct the mistakes in these words?

shoping	_____	restarant	_____
trafic	_____	musuem	_____
betwen	_____	turist	_____
practicing	_____	oposite	_____
admision	_____	art galery	_____

10

Giving opinions

1 Match the first and second parts.

1 It was a brilliant film.
2 It wasn't a bad pizza.
3 It was an awful meal.
4 It was a pretty good book.
5 The concert was a bit disappointing.
6 The exhibition was nothing special.

☐ I thought the orchestra would be much better.
☐ Not the best I've had, but not the worst.
☐ That's the last time I eat there.
☐ Lots of paintings, but none of them much good.
☐ I'd like to read something else by her.
1 I'm going to see it again tomorrow.

Your top five

2 Read this extract from a film magazine.

We want you to have your own page on our web site.

This is what you do. Send us your personal top five list on any film or TV subject you want and, if we choose you, we'll design a page for you with your name and your top five list (with your personal comments, of course) for the whole world to see! Remember, you can choose best films, worst films, soundtracks, music videos, favourite TV programmes … even video games if you want!

Matt's top five film soundtracks

▶ **The Beach** – takes me to hot and sunny places

▶ **Pulp Fiction** – I love Tarantino

▶ **Saturday Night Fever** – terrible hairstyles, but a classic

▶ **The Piano** – remember the piano on the beach?

▶ **Trainspotting** – a brilliant mixture of music

3 Now follow the instructions and write your own 'top five'. If you don't like any of the ideas, choose something you are interested in. Don't forget to add your personal comments.

What was it like?

4 Think about these things:
- the last meal you had in a restaurant
- the last film you saw
- the last book you read
- the last holiday you went on

For each one, answer the question *What was it like?*
You can use these adjectives if you like.

delicious	relaxing	expensive	interesting
awful	luxurious	disappointing	boring

meal _____

film _____

book _____

holiday _____

11

Present continuous (future)

1 Complete the e-mail with the verbs in the box. One of
the verbs is not in the box. Can you think what it is?

is having	are playing	isn't coming	're visiting
is driving	are you flying	's having	

				11.10
From:	Will		**To:**	Jorge
Subject:	Next week			

Message:

Hi there, Jorge

Thanks a lot for your e-mail. Great to hear from
you! So, you ¹ _____ next week. I'm
sorry Ana ² _____ too – maybe next
time. ³ _____ or coming by train? Let
me know.

My brother, Iain, ⁴ _____ a birthday
party at his flat when you're here. All his friends
⁵ _____ , and he ⁶ _____
a disco, so it should be cool. His girlfriend – you
remember Lena, don't you? – ⁷ _____
up from London.

By the way, the Prodigy ⁸ _____ in
Edinburgh on the Saturday. Do you want me to get
tickets?

See you on Thursday.

Will

---

2 Write Jorge's reply to Will's e-mail. Answer his
questions and ask two of your own.

				16.30
From:	Jorge .		**To:**	Will
Subject:	RE: Next week			

Message: Hi Will

---

3 Complete the dialogue with present continuous
questions using the words in (brackets). Use a different
question word for each one. Choose from the list below.

Why	Where	Who	What	How

A ¹ _____ ? (doing / weekend)

B Going to the coast.

A Good idea. ² _____ ? (going with)

B Jan and Petros. Want to come?

A I don't know ... ³ _____ ? (getting there)

B By train probably.

A ⁴ _____ ? (staying)

B I'm not sure. We'll find a B & B or something.
⁵ _____ ? (asking)

A I don't think I can afford it.

Prepositions

4 Put the times, days, months, and dates in the right
column.

Tuesday	4.30
17 November	Wednesday morning
the weekend	Saturday evening
8.30 in the evening	the afternoon
December	early April
midnight	late September

in	on	at

5 What are your plans for the rest of this week / next week? Use time phrases like the ones in exercise 4.

I'm going to the Leeds game on Saturday.

Making plans

6 Three friends are making plans. Put their conversation in the right order.

Mike	Yes, sure. We're leaving here at 8.00. What about you, Ally, are you doing anything?	☐
Tony	Mary is coming up from London tonight. Can we join you? I know she loves Italian food.	☐
Ally	I've got a splitting headache. But thanks for asking, anyway.	☐
Tony	Why? What's wrong?	☐
Mike	I'm going out with Rebecca.	☐
Tony	What are you doing tonight?	☑ 1
Ally	No, I'm staying in. I'm not feeling very well.	☐
Mike	We're meeting Louise and Andrew at Umberto's. It's a great restaurant. The food's excellent.	☐
Ally	Where are you going?	☐

12

Travel announcements

1 What are these announcements? Write them out correctly.

1 thisisaplatformalterationwouldallpassengerswaitingon platform3forthe845tocambridgepleasegotoplatform1

This is a platform alteration. Would all …

2 weapologizeforthelatearrivalofthe1215frommanchester itiscurrently5minuteslateandisduetoarriveat1530

3 thisisachangeofgateflightba0912toparis isnowboardingatgate9

4 allairfranceflightsleavefromterminaltwo

Transport vocabulary

2 Think of the transport you use in these situations and why. Write sentences.

When I go out for the evening I usually take the bus, because I like having a drink. Sometimes I drive if …

1 When I go out for the evening …

2 When I want to visit another town / city …

3 When I go down the road to see a friend or to buy a paper …

4 When I do my weekly shopping …

5 When I travel to another country …

Reading

Read the directions on how to get to these tourist attractions and answer the questions.

Deep-Sea World

Road: Cross the Forth Bridge, take the first exit left, and follow the signs. Free car parking.

Bus: For information on bus services call 01383 621249.

Train: Regular connections from Edinburgh.

The PALACE of HOLYROOD HOUSE

The Palace is easily reached by visitors arriving in Edinburgh by car, train or coach. Waverley Train Station is 15 minutes' walk from the Palace. Coach parking is provided free of charge and the open-top tour buses stop nearby. Local buses numbers 1 and 6 also stop opposite the Palace.

Edinburgh Zoo

By road – the Zoo is 3 miles west of the city centre.

By bus – from the city centre, numbers 2, 12, 26, 31, 36, 69.

By rail – Edinburgh Waverley Station, then any of the above buses.

1 Which place has more buses going to it, the zoo or the palace? How many are there?

2 Where do the local buses going to the Palace of Holyrood House stop?

3 How long does it take to walk from the train station to the Palace?

4 If you decide to drive to the zoo, how far is it from the city centre of Edinburgh?

5 Are there many trains to Deep-Sea World?

6 What is the telephone number for information on buses to Deep-Sea World?

7 Is the train station close enough to the zoo to walk?

8 Do you have to pay to park at Deep-Sea World?

1 Complete the texts with these words.

transport	few	travel	plenty
getting	around	service	expensive

Japan

Train is the best way to ¹_____ – fast, frequent, clean, comfortable (but very expensive!). Motorbikes can also be a great way of getting ²_____ – traffic drives on the left. Ferries connect the main islands with the many smaller islands off the coast. Every city has a bus ³_____ , but it can be difficult for foreigners to use.

2 Which description is most like where you live?

3 Write a short text describing transport in your city or country. Use the texts in exercise 1 to help you.

London

⁴_____ around can be quite expensive. There are ⁵_____ of buses but the traffic is bad – don't bring a car into the centre if you can avoid it! The underground system is large, but it's getting old and can be unreliable. Taxis are ⁶_____ .

Brazil

Flights are not cheap, but with the huge distances, planes are sometimes a necessity. Buses and coaches are the main form of ⁷_____ , and are excellent and cheap. There are very ⁸_____ train services. It is still possible to travel by boat in some areas, especially Amazonia.

Test your spelling lessons 10–12

Two words in each sentence are misspelt. Can you find them and correct them?

1 The exibition was very disapointing.

2 The concert was absolutely briliant.

3 Is accomodation included in the price of the holliday?

4 I'm going out for diner on Wedesday.

5 Busses are cheap and confortable.

13

Present continuous

1 Complete what these people are saying on their mobile phones. Use the verbs in the box.

stand	have	walk	sit

1 I _____ outside the post office.

2 I _____ lunch in Billie's Bistro.

3 I _____ down the High Street. I'm just passing the library.

4 I _____ on a bench in the park.

2 What do you think these people are saying?

3 Look at these two pictures. How are they different? Answer the questions.

1 Where are they?

2 What are they wearing?

3 Who are they talking to?

4 How are they feeling?

5 What are they thinking?

6 What are they saying?

4 Match the two parts of these sentences. Number them in order to make a complete e-mail.

Hi June

☐	I finish college this summer,		job's going well.
☐	I hope your new		after so long.
1	Great to hear from you		because I want to study during the week.
☐	I'm working with my brother		so then I can find a real job.
☐	He needs help		but I've got a new job too!
☐	I'm only working at weekends		in his shop.
☐	You won't believe it,		and I need the money!

That's all for now. Keep in touch!

love Marty

14

Telephone language

1 Look at Tapescript 14.1. Find expressions which mean the same as the ones below.

1	Julia?	*Is that Julia?*
2	This is Julia.	*Yes, speaking.*
3	This is Michael speaking.	_____
4	Can I speak to Robert, please?	_____
5	Do you want me to give him a message?	_____
6	Could he get back to me before 9.00 tonight?	_____
7	OK, I'll just get a pen.	_____
8	What's your number?	_____

Communicating vocabulary

2 Choose the correct word to complete these sentences.

1　A　Do you know Simon's address?
　　B　No, I haven't got my **address book / address list**.

2　A　What's their number?
　　B　I don't know. Look it up in the **phone book / phone list**.

3　Excuse me. Is there a **phone cabin / phone box** near here?

4　What's your e-mail **number / address**?

5　I've got some letters here. Are you going past the **postbox / postbag**?

3 Read the paragraph on alarm calls from the telephone directory. Complete it with the words in the box.

time	alarm	clock	answer
second	evening	rings	called
morning	enter		

Reminder Call

This service turns your phone into an
1 ___*alarm*___ clock. Simply set the
2 _____ using the 24 hour
3 _____ . For example, to be called at
7.30 in the 4 _____ , enter 0730 as the
time, or to be 5 _____ at 7.30 in the
6 _____ , 7 _____ 1930 as
the time. When your call comes through, the
phone 8 _____ several times. If you do
not 9 _____ it, the phone rings again,
but for a 10 _____ time only.

Reading

1 Read the instructions on making emergency calls.

1　What number do you call in an emergency in Britain?

2　What other number can you try?

3　Which emergency service do you ask for if you see a car accident?

4　Which emergency service do you ask for if you see someone having problems in the sea?

2 Complete the questions that the operator might ask in an emergency.

1　Operator　_____ ?
　　Caller　　Flat 2B, 303 Leeds Street.

2　Operator　_____ ?
　　Caller　　There's a fire in our kitchen.

3　Operator　_____ ?
　　Caller　　I'm calling from a neighbour's flat.

Fire

Police

Ambulance

Cave rescue

Mountain rescue

Coastguard *sea and cliff rescue*

1 Lift the handset and **PRESS OR DIAL 999 – 112** may also be used as an alternative to 999.

2 Tell the operator **WHICH EMERGENCY SERVICE YOU WANT**.

3 Wait for the operator to connect you to the Emergency Service.

4 Tell the Emergency Service –

• **WHERE THE TROUBLE IS**
• **WHAT THE TROUBLE IS**
• **WHERE YOU ARE** and the number of the phone you are using.

Writing

Write two replies to this e-mail.

- In the first say yes, and suggest a meeting place and time.
- In the second say no, apologize, and give a reason.

			18.11
From:	Rory	To:	Jim
Subject:	Saturday evening		
Message:	Hi Jim!		
	Cinema on Saturday?		
	Rory		

15

Giving advice

1 Match the problems and the advice.

1 My watch has stopped.

2 I need to be in Edinburgh by 9.00 a.m. on Monday morning.

3 Someone's stolen my wallet!

4 I bought this CD player yesterday and it doesn't work properly.

5 I think my wife has got food poisoning.

6 I haven't got any money left.

- ☐ You should take it back to the shop.
- ☐ You should go to the police.
- ☐ You should take her to the doctor.
- ☐ You should fly.
- ☐ You shouldn't spend so much!
- ☑ You should try putting a new battery in it.

2 Complete these dialogues. Start in three different ways.

1

A How are _____ ?

B Well, actually, not so good. I've got an awful headache.

A Oh dear, you should _____ .

2

A How's _____ ?

B Not great. I forgot our wedding anniversary today.

A Oh no! You should _____ .

3

A How _____ ?

B Could be better. My car broke down again this morning.

A Oh? Perhaps you should _____ .

Feelings

3 Complete these sentences – make them true for you.

I feel relaxed ... *when the sun is shining*.

1 I feel fed up when ...

2 I feel happy when ...

3 I feel excited when ...

4 I get upset when ...

5 I feel tired when ...

16

Food

1 Label the picture.

bananas	peas	grapes	cabbage
plums	onions	oranges	carrots
cauliflower	beans	apples	avocado

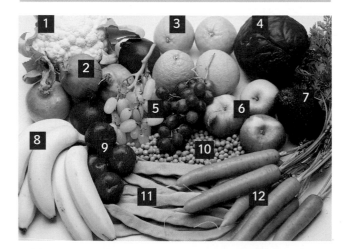

2 Add two more things to the list in exercise 1.

3 Put different food or drink in each column.

I love	I don't mind	I can't stand

In a restaurant

4 Match the questions a waiter asks to the situations.

Waiter's questions

1 Are you ready to order?
2 Would you like something to drink?
3 Coffee?
4 Anything else?
5 Smoking or non-smoking?
6 Would you like some dessert?

Situations

5 When you first arrive in the restaurant
☐ Before you look at the menu.
☐ After you look at the menu.
☐ After you finish ordering your starter and your main course.
☐ After you finish eating your main course.
☐ After your meal.

5 Now match the waiter's questions to these answers. (Sometimes there is more than one possibility.)

3 Yes, please, black.
☐ Not quite.
☐ Yes, I'll have mineral water, please.
☐ Not for me, thanks.
☐ Um, yes ... a green salad, please.
☐ Smoking, please.
☐ Yes, we are.
☐ No, thanks, can we just have the bill, please?

6 What's the most useful question for you to know in a restaurant? Make a polite question that you can use with all these things.

the menu?
_____ more wine?
a bottle of water?
the bill?

Countable and uncountable nouns

7 Countable and uncountable nouns aren't just for food. Are these nouns countable (**C**) or uncountable (**U**)?

furniture	☐	hair	☐
information	☐	luggage	☐
money	☐	news	☐
problem	☐	advice	☐

8 Complete these sentences with the correct form of the verb in (brackets).

1 The furniture in that shop _____ (not / be) very good quality.
2 How heavy _____ (be) your luggage?
3 That information you gave me _____ (be) so useful.
4 My hair _____ (feel) dirty.
5 The news _____ (not / be) very good, I'm afraid.
6 Money _____ (not / grow) on trees.

9 Make four sentences with the other nouns in exercise 7.

Reading

1 Read the text about restaurants in Russia. Are these sentences true (✓) or false (✗)?

1 There are lots of restaurants in Moscow. ☐
2 Prices are always very high. ☐
3 Small towns also have a lot of restaurants. ☐
4 Restaurants stay open in the afternoon. ☐
5 All restaurants have music and dancing. ☐
6 It's a good idea to make a reservation. ☐

2 These adjectives are all in the text. Which nouns go with each one?

high	prices
private	
traditional	
energetic	
loud	
affordable	

3 Find another noun for each adjective. Use a dictionary to help you.

Moscow and St Petersburg are full of private cafés and restaurants offering everything from pizza to Indian, French, and Chinese food. Prices are often extremely high. Restaurants in smaller towns are rare, but increasing in number. For a full meal, you can go anywhere from the most basic canteen to a proper restaurant. In general, restaurants open from mid-morning to about 11 p.m. or midnight, usually with a break for a couple of hours in the afternoon. Russians like to relax in the evening, with loud music and energetic dancing in traditional Russian restaurants. Good affordable restaurants are usually full in the evenings, so book early.

17

Restaurant vocabulary

1 Match these words and pictures.

a knife
a fork
a spoon
a wine glass
a jug
a bottle
salt and pepper
chopsticks
the bill

Booking a table

2 Complete the other half of this phone conversation.

Waiter	Hello, the Star of India.
Customer	_____
Waiter	When would that be for?
Customer	_____
Waiter	For how many?
Customer	_____
Waiter	Yes, that will be fine. Could I take a name and phone number?
Customer	_____
Waiter	Thank you. We'll see you then.

18

Past simple

1 Look at Tapescripts 18.1 and 18.2 and write questions for these answers.

1 *What film did Vic and Sarah see?*
   Go.

2 _____ ?
   He did, but she didn't.

3 _____ ?
   In the pub.

4 _____ ?
   Fish pie.

5 _____ ?
   A CD.

6 _____ ?
   Because it was his birthday.

7 _____ ?
   About 9.30.

8 _____ ?
   It was horrible.

2 Complete the crossword. One answer is not a past simple verb – which one?

across →

1 I r*ang* her at 10.00 last night.
4 You _____ what I said, didn't you?
7 It was sunny in the morning, but then it _____ to rain.
9 I _____ too much dinner last night.
11 She _____ French and Spanish at a secondary school.
14 I _____ the washing-up.
15 I _____ my wallet yesterday – and it had all my credit cards in it.
18 'Was that pen expensive?' 'No, it _____ about 80p.'
20 I _____ him but I couldn't remember his name.
22 She _____ a blue dress.

down ↓

1 Last year I _____ in the New York marathon.
2 There was an accident here yesterday – a car _____ a cyclist.
3 I _____ £10 in the street this morning.
5 I didn't take the bus, I _____ .
6 I _____ a noise and got out of bed.
7 I _____ two new suits in the sales.
8 My parents _____ me a CD player for my birthday.
10 He _____ me two letters last month.
12 I went to Italy two years _____ .
13 I _____ the bus to work this morning.
14 We _____ two glasses of red wine.
16 His English wasn't very good, so we _____ Spanish.
17 'Did you come by train?' 'No, I _____ .'
19 She _____ me an interesting story.
21 I _____ £250 in the lottery last week.

3 Write six sentences about what you did last weekend. Use the verbs in the box, and use *didn't* for two sentences.

go	buy	see	visit
write	have	enjoy	meet

4 Read this postcard. Put the verbs in (brackets) in the past simple. One is negative.

Dear Will

I wanted to thank you for a great weekend and I ¹_____ (choose) this card because I really ²_____ (like) the picture. It ³_____ (remind) me of the concert we ⁴_____ (go) to with your brother and his girlfriend.

Actually, we ⁵_____ (go) to another concert last night, but it ⁶_____ (be) very different. My parents ⁷_____ (take) Ana and me to see Buddy Guy. I ⁸_____ (think) I liked blues, but it wasn't too bad. My parents loved it, but Ana ⁹_____ (hate) it – in fact, she ¹⁰_____ (leave) at the interval and really ¹¹_____ (upset) my parents. The worst thing was that they ¹²_____ (pay) for it!

I ¹³_____ (phone) her this afternoon, but I only ¹⁴_____ (get) the answering machine. My parents don't want to see her again! Help! Any ideas?

Well, that's all for now. Hope things are going well with you. E-mail me when you have time.

Jorge

Writing

Write an e-mail to Jorge with some advice on what to do about Ana and his parents.

	10.10
From: _____	To: Jorge
Subject:	Ana and your parents
Message:	Dear Jorge
	It sounds like a difficult situation …

-ed pronunciation

5 Write the past simple of these verbs in the right column.

remember	repeat	close	listen
change	cook	book	dance
end	love	like	look

opened	finished	started

last and ago

6 Answer these questions about yourself.

1 Where did you go on holiday last year?
2 Where were you a week ago?
3 What was the most exciting thing you did last weekend?
4 What did you have for dinner last night?
5 What was the most interesting news you heard or read last week?
6 What was the worst film you saw last year?
7 Where did you live five years ago?
8 Do you speak better English now than you did a couple of months ago?

The number '0'

7 Look at *p.56*. How do you say 40–0 in a game of tennis? Match these numbers with the descriptions. How can you say '0' in each one?

3–0	temperature	nought
0%	telephone number	nil
0°	interest rates	oh
305 7088	football score	zero

8 Write a sentence using the word *nothing*.

Test your spelling lessons 16–18

Write these words in full.

cmptr = *computer*

pzz	_____	clths	_____
vgtbls	_____	pppr	_____
frdg	_____	sndwch	_____
xpnsv	_____	brthdy	_____

19

Comparative adjectives

1 Put the words in these sentences in order. Make each one true for you and give a reason.

out is relaxing than home more eating eating at
Eating out is more relaxing than eating at home because ...
or
Eating at home is more relaxing than eating out because ...

1 train than bus by is travelling better by
2 than like evenings I mornings better
3 more I in a jeans than in suit comfortable feel
4 living the than is country the better in living city in
5 convenient a in in house more living flat than living a is
6 working a easier student is than being

2 Write three more sentences about your opinions. Use adjectives from the box.

I think trains are more comfortable than buses.

bad	happy	exciting	crowded
comfortable	quiet	clean	beautiful

3 How much do you know about the world? Are these statements true (✓) or false (✗)?

1 Russia is bigger than China.

2 More people speak Portuguese than Spanish.

3 New York is further north than Moscow.

4 Los Angeles is hotter than San Francisco.

5 Scotland has higher mountains than Wales.

6 New Zealand has more sheep than people.

7 More people speak Japanese than Chinese.

8 Spain is more mountainous than any other country in Europe.

4 Compare these countries in as many ways as you can. When you compare two countries, draw a line between them.

Tanzania is larger than Iceland.

Saudi Arabia

Iceland

Greece

Argentina

Tanzania

Russia

China

Australia

20

Airport and in-flight vocabulary

1 Complete the words. The missing letters are all vowels (*a, e, i, o, u*).

ch__ck-__n   __c__n__my cl__ss

b__ard__ng p__ss   b__s__n__ss cl__ss

f__rst cl__ss   d__p__rt__r__ lo__ng__

s__ngl__   g__t__

__rriv__l h__ll   p__ssp__rt c__ntr__l

r__und tr__p   b__gg__g__ r__cl__im

Booking a flight

2 Match the questions and the answers.

1 How many people are travelling?

2 When do you want to travel?

3 Single or return?

4 How would you like to pay?

5 What's the card number?

6 What's the expiry date?

☐ Return, please.

☐ 3969 7854 3555 3212.

☐ Two adults and two children.

☐ Credit card, please.

☐ August 2007.

☐ Next Saturday.

Reading

1 Look at this ASS Travel Insurance 'Deluxe Plan' and answer the questions.

Deluxe plan coverage	Limit
Trip cancellation or interruption	£1,000
Travel delay (£100 max. per day)	£300
Baggage and travel documents	£500
Baggage delay	£100
Medical expense	£10,000
Emergency medical transportation	£20,000
Flight accident	£200,000
Total policy fee per year (per person)	**£305**

1 How much does the plan cost for a couple for one year?

2 What is the maximum you get if …

• you lose your passport?

• your plane is delayed?

• you need an ambulance?

• there is a plane crash?

• you have to go to hospital?

2 Read what a customer of ASS Travel Insurance said. Mark the sentences true (✓), false (✗) or don't know (?).

While on holiday in the West Indies, Gloria fell down some steps and hit her head. After a visit to the local doctor, we soon realized that the injury was serious, and that we needed outside assistance. I decided to call ASS Travel Insurance. I wanted advice, but I got more than that. A medical team arrived in no time and flew us to Miami in less than eight hours. The neuro-surgeon told me that my wife was close to death. However, she recovered and we are now looking forward to travelling again. And we have your company to thank. I now tell all my friends to buy ASS Travel Insurance. Thanks again.

1 The couple live in the West Indies. ☐

2 The man had an accident. ☐

3 The local doctor was American. ☐

4 The local doctor couldn't help. ☐

5 A team of doctors arrived very quickly. ☐

6 It took eight hours to get back to Miami. ☐

7 The wife's injury was extremely serious. ☐

8 It took months for her to get better. ☐

9 All the man's friends have the same insurance plan. ☐

10 This man thinks ASS Travel Insurance is a good deal. ☐

3 Underline the past simple verbs in the text, and put them in the right column. Include the infinitives.

regular	irregular
	fall / fell

4 The verb *hit* is the same in the present and the past. Look at the irregular verbs on *p.111*. Which other verbs do not change their spelling?

present ⟹ past

hit   hit

21

Hotels and accommodation

1 Answer these questions and write the first letter of each answer to find a kind of holiday accommodation.

1 *p.26* The Natural History Museum is in this road.
2 *p.23* She likes black and white films.
3 *p.08* She writes Jim an e-mail.
4 *p.53* The name of the restaurant on Nicholson Street.
5 *p.11* The name of Rita's daughter.
6 *p.17* She lives in the Solomon Islands.
7 *p.40* He's working at Pizza Rapide.
8 *p.04* Maria's surname.
9 *p.32* The police constable's first name.

1	2	3	4	5	6	7	8	9

2 Complete the gaps in this dialogue.

A Hello, York Hotel.
B Hello, I *'d* _____ _____ _____ book a _____ for this Wednesday, please.
A Certainly, sir. What _____ _____ room _____ _____ like?
B A single with en suite _____ , please.
A Yes, _____ _____ _____ single free.
B Could you tell me _____ _____ _____ _____ ?
A It's £85.
B _____ _____ _____ breakfast?
A Yes, it does.
B OK. Can I _____ _____ later to confirm?
A Yes, of course.

Reading

1 Compare these descriptions of hotels in Bangkok and Helsinki and answer the questions. <u>Underline</u> the parts that tell you the answers.

1 Which hotel is better for people who don't like smoking? *Anta Hotel*
2 Which hotel doesn't have a restaurant?
3 Which hotel is better for people who like swimming?
4 What kind of guests does the Anta Hotel want?
5 Which hotel is closer to the airport?
6 Name one facility found in the Anta Hotel, but not in the Grace Hotel.
7 What kind of food does the Grace Hotel offer?
8 Which hotel lets you send faxes from your room?

2 Find the opposites of these adjectives in the hotel descriptions.

unfriendly   _____
indoor   _____
ugly   _____
uncomfortable   _____
cold   _____
unknown   _____
local   _____

Grace Hotel
Bangkok

Anta Hotel
Helsinki

The Grace Hotel is an attractive hotel located in the centre of one of the business and shopping areas of Bangkok. Our luxury guest rooms are comfortable and offer air-conditioning, mini-bar, colour TV with video, telephone, personal safe and facsimile machine. There is a lobby bar, coffee shop, restaurant offering Thai, Chinese and international food, and an outdoor pool. The International Airport is just 10 kilometres away.

The Anta Hotel is a welcoming hotel situated in the centre of the city. The cosy, attractive hotel has got <u>a whole floor for non-smokers</u>. Personal service and a warm atmosphere are ideal for both business and leisure guests. All rooms have air-conditioning, mini-bar, TV and telephone. There is a sauna and hotel bar. The vicinity has a number of famous restaurants offering all kinds of cuisine. The hotel is just 20 km from Helsinki–Vantaa International Airport.

3 Where did these people stay on holiday? Use the words in the box.

| camp-site | hotel | guest-house |
| camper van | self-catering apartment | |

1 *We wanted something like a hotel, but not as expensive.*

2 *We wanted a bed to sleep in, but we also wanted to cook for ourselves.*

3 *We wanted to tour around by ourselves.*

4 *We wanted to try out our tent.*

5 *I wanted comfort, and everything on a plate.*

Test your spelling lessons 19–21

One word in each sentence is misspelt. Can you find it and correct it?

1 The countryside is very mountanous.

2 I really don't like big citys.

3 The wether's really cloudy.

4 I think camping's unconfortable.

5 There are too many advertisments on television.

22

Present perfect

1 Put the words in the right order to make sentences.

1 haven't before flown they
They haven't flown before.

2 ? you been ever Edinburgh have to

_____

3 any never money won I've

_____

4 studied I before English haven't

_____

5 Kathryn times have how you ? many met

_____

6 bought she a has car ? before

_____

7 have Russell been hasn't to but Tokyo I

_____

8 times seen that we've three film

_____

Present perfect and past simple

2 Choose the correct form of the verb.

1 **I've been / I went** to the theatre twice this week.

2 Mike and Jenny **have come / came** for dinner last weekend.

3 **We have never visited / We never visited** Mexico before.

4 **Have you ever seen / Did you ever see** *Pulp Fiction*?

5 How often **have you had / did you have** a real Italian pizza?

6 **I have saved / I saved** enough money to go on holiday to France last year.

7 A Did you have a good time?
   B Yes, **I have / I did**.

8 Atlético Bilbao **have won / won** the championship last night.

3 Write down five things you've never done that you'd like to do one day.
I've never been hang-gliding.

Money vocabulary

4 Each sentence has an anagram of a 'money' word in it. Write the word correctly and complete the sentence with a preposition from the box.

| by | from | to | in | for |

1 You can _____ (RROWOB) money _____ me if you need it.

2 Can I _____ (YPA) _____ credit card?

3 Have you got _____ (HGCNAE) _____ a pound?

4 Don't _____ (DNLE) money _____ Jake. He never pays you back.

5 I'm _____ (ISVAGN) _____ a holiday this summer, but I always seem to _____ (DSENP) as fast as I _____ (NRAE).

6 How do you want to pay? _____ _____ (QUCHEE), _____ _____ (RDITEC DARC), or _____ _____ (SHAC)?

5 What is expensive and what is cheap in your country? Try to write three things in each column.

cheap	average	expensive
		eating out

6 Now write five sentences about prices in your country.
*Public transport is **cheap**, especially if you buy a travel card. Eating out can be very **expensive**.*

Read this extract from a travel guide and choose the best answer for the questions.

> You can exchange money officially at all hotels and banks. However, remember you can only sell foreign currency. You cannot buy it back, so only change what you need. American dollars are the easiest currency to change.
>
> If you need to transfer money from abroad, American Express (office in the main square) is the easiest way. You can also send cash via any post office, usually within 24 hours.
>
> Most hotels, many shops and the better restaurants accept major credit cards. Banks will cash traveller's cheques, but the commission can be high.
>
> Make sure you have enough money for the weekend. The banks are closed, and some hotels will tell you to wait till Monday.

1 You can change money ...
  • in hotels and banks.
  • only in banks.
  • only in hotels.

2 The guide advises readers ...
  • to buy lots of local currency.
  • not to buy local currency.
  • to buy no more local currency than necessary.

3 Tourists can use credit cards in ...
  • all restaurants.
  • more expensive restaurants.
  • hotel restaurants only.

4 Banks ...
  • sometimes charge you a large commission for changing traveller's cheques.
  • charge you a small commission for changing traveller's cheques.
  • don't change traveller's cheques.

5 You can change money in banks ...
  • at any time.
  • at weekends only.
  • on weekdays only.

23

Describing things

1 Look at the pictures. Where can you buy each of the objects? Write the name of the shop next to each one.

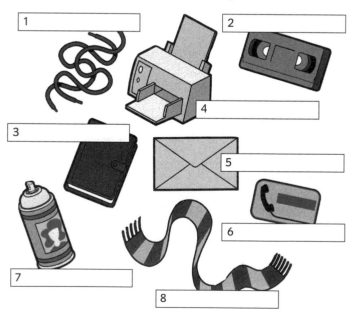

2 Choose three objects you don't know the name of in English. Look up the words in a dictionary and write a short description of each.

video tapes

They're for recording films or TV programmes, and you can buy them in a music shop or in some large supermarkets.

Internet shopping

3 Read this article. Are you the same as Nicola?

Nicola Murphy has already started doing her Christmas shopping on the Internet. She usually spends about £300 on presents and pays for them on her debit card. The 35-year-old sales manager is buying food and drink from supermarket shopping services and has ordered books and CDs from on-line bookshops.

'Buying over the Internet saves me a lot of money,' says Nicola, 'and it's a lot nicer staying at home than having to go out in the High Street. I only buy from well-known companies.'

Nicola also likes the fact that she doesn't have to take her two children, Sally (3) and Lisa (6) around the supermarket with her. 'I sit down in the evening, check the cupboards in the kitchen, and prepare my shopping list,' she says. 'I very rarely forget things any more.'

4 Write questions for these answers from the text. Use these question words to help you.

- ## When?
- ## How?
- ## Which?
- ## How much?
- ## Why?

1 *Why does Nicola like Internet shopping?*
Because it saves a lot of money.

2 _____ ?
About £300.

3 _____ ?
In the evening.

4 _____ ?
35.

5 _____ ?
Only well-known ones.

6 _____ ?
She doesn't have to take her young children to the supermarket.

Writing

1 Nicola only talks about the advantages of Internet shopping. Put them in the table. What do you think are the disadvantages?

2 What do you think about Internet shopping? Use the ideas in the table, and write a paragraph.
I think Internet shopping is …

advantages	disadvantages
It saves a lot of money.	

24

Clothes vocabulary

1 Complete the spidergram with these clothes and accessories. Add another item to each box.

jeans	trainers	gloves	a suit
T-shirts	make-up	shorts	sandals
a watch	a ring	sunglasses	bright colours

I always wear …

I often wear…

CLOTHES

I sometimes wear…

I never wear…

Your country and Britain

2 How much do you know about clothes? Answer these questions for your country and for Britain.

1 Do men and women usually wear hats to a wedding?
2 Do visitors take their shoes off when they come into the house?
3 Do people take their hats off in a religious place?
4 Do businesspeople always wear a suit to work?
5 Do people wear shorts in the city?
6 Do women wear short sleeves?
7 Do women wear trousers?
8 Do male teachers always wear ties to work?
9 Do women wear white to get married?
10 Do women wear black when they lose their husbands?

In my country	In Britain
1	1 *Men sometimes do, women usually do.*
2	2
3	3
4	4
5	5
6	6
7	7

Read this description of Scottish traditional dress and label the photograph.

The tartan kilt has long been the traditional dress in Scotland. Different tartans belong to different clans or families. The first time that everyone in a clan started to wear the same tartan was in 1618. One of the most famous tartans is the Black Watch Tartan, which was designed in 1740 especially for the Black Watch regiment. The modern kilt that we can see today was made in the 1800s. It is not as big and heavy as the original kilt or 'philabeg', as it was called. Nowadays, all Scots can find the tartan for their own clan or family.

Scotsmen traditionally wear the kilt with a jacket, a white shirt, thick socks and black leather shoes. Round their waists they wear a sporran (a kind of purse) and in one sock they wear a traditional dirk (a small knife). On their heads they sometimes wear a beret. Women wear tartan too, but not with a sporran or a dirk. Many wear a simple white dress with a tartan plaid.

Nowadays, you don't see kilts every day, but men still wear them for weddings, dances, and rugby matches.

Writing

What is the traditional costume in your country? Is it different for men and women? When do people wear these clothes? Write a short description of the costume. You can draw a simple picture to help you, or find a photograph.

Test your spelling lessons 22–24

Can you correct the mistakes in these words?

borow	_____	fleace	_____
scisors	_____	breifcase	_____
apointment	_____	bacpack	_____
charety	_____	shoping	_____
siut	_____	coffe	_____

PAIR WORK ACTIVITIES

09 ROADS & ROUNDABOUTS

Student A

Look at your map. You want to find these places.

- a Chinese restaurant
- a music shop
- a café
- a photographic shop
- a camping shop
- a newsagent

Ask your partner questions and mark the places on the map. Try to use different questions.

Excuse me, is there a (good) _____ near here?

Do you know if there's a (good) _____ around here?

Do you know where there's a (good) _____ ?

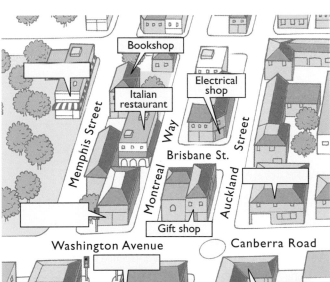

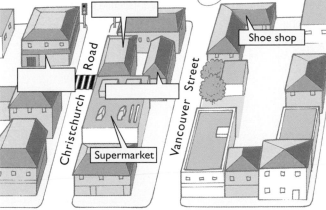

14 CALLS & MESSAGES

Student A

CLUBCARDS

RICHARD SCRANNAGE
DIRECTOR

CLUBCARDS LTD	TEL _____
9 _____	FAX _____
LONDON	E-MAIL _____
SW _____	WWW. _____

**ED Diana Berry
Endplate Design**

2704 17th Avenue	telephone (403) 686-2455
Calgary	fax (403) 686-2456
Alberta	berryd@endplate.com
AB T3N 2V6	www.endplatedesign.com

21 SINGLES & DOUBLES

Student A

You want to book a hotel room in Cape Town. Decide what you want and complete the table.

| How many people are in your group? _____ |
| What type(s) of room do you need? _____ |
| When are you arriving? _____ |
| When are you leaving? _____ |

Decide what you want the hotel to offer – choose three things:

- breakfast included ☐
- conference facilities ☐
- a minibar in the room ☐
- a gym ☐
- a casino ☐
- a sauna ☐
- a choice of restaurants ☐
- close to city centre ☐
- satellite TV ☐

09 ROADS & ROUNDABOUTS

Student B

Look at your map. You want to find these places.

- a shoe shop
- a gift shop
- a supermarket
- a bookshop
- an Italian restaurant
- an electrical shop

Ask your partner questions and mark the places on the map. Try to use different questions.

Excuse me, is there a (good) _____ near here?

Do you know if there's a (good) _____ around here?

Do you know where there's a (good) _____ ?

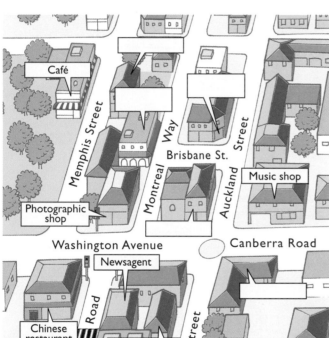
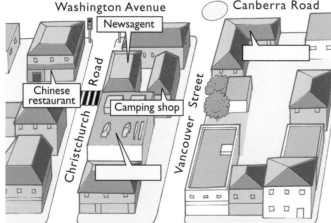

14 CALLS & MESSAGES

Student B

CLUBCARDS LTD	TEL 020 8540 9111
9 LYON ROAD	FAX 020 8543 5115
LONDON	E-MAIL DICK@CLUBCARDS.CO.UK
SW19 2RL	WWW.CLUBCARDS.COM

ED

Diana Berry
Endplate Design

2704 _____	telephone _____
Calgary	fax _____
Alberta	berryd@_____
AB_____	www._____

21 SINGLES & DOUBLES

Student B

You run a busy hotel in Cape Town. Complete the table.

How many rooms have you got free?
(singles / doubles / twins)

_____

How much do the rooms cost per night?

_____

What's included in the price?

_____

What facilities does your hotel offer? Choose three things:

a minibar in the room	☐	conference facilities	☐
a casino	☐	a gym	☐
a choice of restaurants	☐	a sauna	☐
satellite TV	☐	close to city centre	☐

TAPESCRIPTS

01 LETTERS & NUMBERS

◉1
1 You can get me in the office on 01864 665207.
2 It's the fifth.
3 It's 147.
4 26.
5 0794 5663661.
6 The ninth of July.

◉2
1 A What's your phone number?
   B You can get me in the office on 01864 665207.
2 A What's the date today?
   B It's the fifth.
3 A How old are you?
   B 26.
4 A What's your mobile phone number?
   B 0794 5663661.
5 A What's your house number?
   B It's 147.
6 A When's your birthday?
   B The ninth of July.

03 FRIENDS & RELATIONS

◉1
Diana
I live in a house in a village near Oxford. It's about 80 years old and made of stone. We've got a living room, study, dining room, and kitchen downstairs. Upstairs there are three bedrooms and two bathrooms – one of them is en suite. I think my favourite room has to be our bedroom – it has a view of the garden and the hills beyond. My husband and I love gardening, so we spend a lot of time outside in the summer.

Shawn
My apartment is on the third floor of an old wooden house. It's pretty big for one person, but that's good. It's got two bedrooms and a very large living room, which is great for me because I travel a lot and bring lots of things home with me. There's a small kitchen with a balcony leading off of it, and a decent bathroom. My favorite room's the living room. That's where I watch TV and listen to music. It's also where the air-conditioning is – it gets hot in Boston in the summer.

04 LIFE & ROUTINE

◉1
1 I usually get up at about 6.30. I just have coffee for breakfast. I get the bus to work. If I'm late I take a taxi, which is a bit expensive. My wife goes by bike, she likes to keep fit.
2 I always go to the gym at lunchtimes, about 12.30 or 12.45. I have a shower there too, and I often go to the café for lunch.
3 I leave the office at around 6.00 and maybe meet some friends for a drink. I don't watch much telly, too much to do, and I never go to bed before midnight.

05 PEOPLE & PLACES

◉1
1 She teaches university students.
2 She goes to work at 8.30.
3 She washes her hair every morning.
4 She studies French and German.
5 She misses her family.

06 JOBS & WORK

◉1
1 A What do you do?
   B I'm a doctor.
2 A What do you do?
   B I work for a publishing company.
3 A What do you do?
   B I'm a teacher in a primary school.

07 LOVE & HATE

◉1
1 I love eating out at the weekend.
2 I can't stand doing nothing.
3 I really like watching TV in the evenings.
4 I quite like clubbing.
5 I hate reading the paper.

◉2
1 I love windsurfing ... the sea, the fresh air ...
2 Sometimes I just like sitting around, doing nothing.
3 I can't stand noisy pubs. I can never hear people.
4 I quite enjoy being alone. I don't always need company.
5 I hate getting up when it's still dark.
6 I quite like watching football on the box, but I prefer being there.
7 I don't like gardening. It hurts my back.
8 I really hate the weather here. It's so depressing.

09 ROADS & ROUNDABOUTS

◉1
1 A Could you tell me where the museum is, please?
   B Yeah, it's near the roundabout.
2 A Is there a Chinese restaurant near here?
   B Yes, it's on that side street, near the traffic lights.
3 A Excuse me. Is there a post office near here?
   B Yes, there's one just down there, between the lights and the shopping centre.
4 A Excuse me, is the art gallery near here?
   B Yes, it's there, on the corner.
5 A Excuse me, is this the way to the Italian restaurant?
   B Yes, keep going, it's next to the bridge.
6 A Could you tell me where the cinema is, please?
   B Do you know the museum? It's opposite there.
7 A Excuse me, do you know if there's a chemist's near here?
   B Yes, there's one in that big shopping centre.
8 A Is there a supermarket near here?
   B Yes, it's on this main road, on the left.
   A Sorry?
   B Just down here, on the left.

◉2
Could you tell me where the bus station is?
Excuse me, is there a post office near here?

10 GOOD & BAD

◉1
1 It was really good. I read it in a week.
2 I thought it was disappointing. I usually like thrillers, but this was boring. And three hours was much too long.
3 The food was really good, but it cost over £40, which is a lot.
4 It was nothing special – the café was better than the paintings!
5 I thought it was awful – I gave up on page 20.
6 It was absolutely fantastic – I love Cuban music.

◉2
1 A What did you think of the book?
   B It was really good.
2 A How was the film?
   B I thought it was disappointing.
3 A What was the restaurant like last night?
   B Well, the food was really good ...
4 A How was that exhibition you went to?
   B It was nothing special.
5 A How was the book?
   B I thought it was awful ...
6 A What was the concert like?
   B It was absolutely fantastic.

◉3
1 It was really good.
2 I thought it was disappointing.
3 The food was really good ...
4 It was nothing special.
5 I thought it was awful ...
6 It was absolutely fantastic.

11 OUT & ABOUT

◉1
Conversation 1
A What are you doing this weekend?
B Oh, nothing much. Shopping, maybe, and a bit of telly.
A Well, if you feel like it, Bella and I are going out for dinner on Saturday, and you'd be more than welcome to come.
B That sounds great – where are you going?
A That Italian place, Umberto's. The food's really excellent. We're meeting Keith there about 8.00. Do you know where it is?
B No, I don't actually.

A Well, we're driving so we can pick you up. About 7.45?
B OK. See you then.

Conversation 2
A What are you doing this weekend?
B We're going to Paris! Jane saw a special offer, £69 all in, so we thought let's go for it.
A Fantastic! When are you leaving?
B We're getting the train on Friday evening, at 7.30.
A And is everything included? Accommodation and everything?
B Yeah, but we're not staying anywhere nice, I don't think. But anything's OK for £69!
A Absolutely. Well, have a great time. And we'll see you on Monday.
B OK. See you then.

2
1 I'm meeting Mary for a coffee.
2 I'm going to a Chinese restaurant with some friends.
3 Staying in and watching TV.
4 Nothing special.
5 I'm going down to London for the day.
6 I'm spending a couple of days with my parents.

3
1 A What are you doing after this lesson?
  B I'm meeting Mary for a coffee.
2 A What are you doing for dinner tonight?
  B I'm going to a Chinese restaurant with some friends.
3 A What are you doing this evening?
  B Staying in and watching TV.
4 A What are you doing tomorrow evening?
  B Nothing special.
5 A What are you doing on Saturday?
  B I'm going down to London for the day.
6 A What are you doing this weekend?
  B I'm spending a couple of days with my parents.

12 TRANSPORT & TRAVEL

1
1 A Could you stop here, please?
  B Sure.
  A How much is that?
  B £5.40, please.
  A Here you are. Keep the change. And could I have a receipt, please?
2 A Excuse me. Is this the train to Glasgow?
  B Yeah, it is.
  A What time does it get there?
  B 6.33.
3 A Can I help you?
  B Yes, I want to go to Dublin this weekend. What's the best way to get there?
  A Well, there are lots of cheap flights at the moment, in fact we've got a special offer …
4 A The city centre, please.
  B That's 75p.
  A Sorry, how much did you say?
  B 75.
5 A A return to London, please.
  B That's £27.50. It'll be £16.00 if you can wait till 9.00.
  A It's OK, I need to travel now.
  B OK, that's £27.50 then, please.

2
a A Is the flight direct?
  B No, you have to change in Singapore.
b A How long is the journey?
  B Two and a half hours.

c A What's the best way to get there?
  B Probably by taxi.
d A Is it better to fly or go by train?
  B It depends – flying's much faster.
e A Could you stop here, please?
  B Yes, sure.
f A Do I need to change?
  B No, it's direct.
g A How much is that?
  B £27.50.
h A How far is it?
  B About 50 miles.
i A Where does the bus leave from?
  B The central bus station.
j A Is this the bus for London?
  B No, you want the blue one over there.
k A What time do we get there?
  B Just after 11.00.
l A How often do the buses go to the city centre?
  B Every ten minutes or so.

3
1 This is a platform alteration. Would all passengers waiting on platform 7 for the 10.30 to Paddington please go to platform 5? Platform 5 for the 10.30 to Paddington.
2 GNER apologizes for the late arrival of the 12.15 from London King's Cross. It is currently 35 minutes behind schedule and is due to arrive at 17.15.
3 Flight BA1462 to Newcastle is now boarding at gate A34. Gate A34 for BA1462 to Newcastle.
4 All Qantas and British Airways flights leave from terminal four.
5 … and we'll be coming round with drinks and a light snack. Our flight time today is about 55 minutes, so we should be arriving at around 2.30 local time.

13 HERE & NOW

1
1 *You have one message. Please wait.*
  Hi, it's me. I'm on the train. We're just leaving the station, and it's still raining. The train's really busy tonight, but at least it's not late, so I should be home soon. I'm having a burger right now, so don't worry about dinner. Love you.
2 *You have no old messages and one new message.*
  Hi, it's Michael. I'm having a couple of beers in the pub with John, so I'll be home a little late. Keep the dinner warm! Bye.
3 *You have one new message.*
  Hi, just me. We're on our way back now. Mary wants to pop into the supermarket first. Just what I need … my feet are killing me. Can you get in a pizza? Thanks. Bye.

14 CALLS & MESSAGES

1
Julia   Hello?
Michael Hello? Is that Julia?
Julia   Yes, speaking.
Michael It's Michael here. Is Robert there?
Julia   No, sorry. He's at the gym. Can I take a message?
Michael Yes, please. It's about the meeting tomorrow. Can he phone me back before 9.00 tonight? I'm going out then.
Julia   OK, just let me get a pen. Right … he's to phone you back before 8.00.
Michael No, before 9.00. I'll be in till 9.00.
Julia   Sorry, before 9.00. What number can he call you on?

Michael 224 6785.
Julia   224 6785. Fine.
Michael If he can't do that, I'll be at home until 8.30 tomorrow morning.
Julia   OK. Before 9.00 tonight or 8.30 tomorrow morning.
Michael Great. Thanks, Julia. Bye.
Julia   OK. Bye.

2
Deirdre Hello?
Jim   Hello, is that Deirdre?
Deirdre Yes, speaking.
Jim   It's Jim. Is George there?
Deirdre No, I'm sorry. He's at the library. Can I take a message?
Jim   Yes, please. It's about our meeting tomorrow. Can he phone me back before 7.00 this evening? I'm going out then.
Deirdre OK, just let me get a pen. Right … before 7.00. What number can he get you on?
Jim   334 6885.
Deirdre That's 334 6885. Fine.
Jim   Great. Thanks, Deirdre. Bye.
Deirdre OK. Bye.

15 UPS & DOWNS

1
1 How are you doing?
2 How's life?
3 How are things?
4 How are you?
5 How's it going?

2
1 A How are you doing?
  B Not so bad, thanks.
2 A How's life?
  B Great!
3 A How are things?
  B Not so good, really.
4 A How are you?
  B Fine, thanks.
5 A How's it going?
  B Could be better.

3
1 *The sea.*
2 Thank you for waiting.
3 *A dog whimpering.*
4 *At the dentist* – Open wide … wider.
5 *Classical music.*
6 You have exactly three hours. The exam starts now.
7 Will you marry me?

4
1 A Are you all right? You look a bit fed up.
  B Yes, I am.
  A What's wrong?
  B I'm trying to send an important e-mail and my computer keeps crashing.
2 A You don't look very happy. What's the matter?
  B Oh, I've got an exam today and I'm so nervous. I really don't feel very well.
3 A How are you?
  B Fine, thanks.
  A You don't look fine. You look worried.
  B Well, yeah, I'm a bit stressed about work right now and I get very tired working so late.
4 A Wow! *You* look excited!
  B Mm! I am. Feeling *very* happy, in fact!
  A Well, come on. Tell me!
  B Jake's asked me to marry him!

5

A How are you?
B Fine, thanks.
A You don't look fine. You look worried.
B Well, yeah, I'm a bit stressed about work right now and I get very tired working so late.
A I think it's crazy. You should talk to your boss about how you feel, and you shouldn't work so many hours. You've got a life to live!

6

A You don't look very happy. What's the matter?
B Oh, I've got an exam today and I'm so nervous. I really don't feel very well.
A Maybe you should take some aspirin and go to bed for an hour.

17 CAFÉS & RESTAURANTS

1

Waiter Hello, Caprice.
Customer Hello, I'd like to book a table, please.
Waiter Certainly, when for?
Customer This evening, about 8.30.
Waiter How many people?
Customer Six.
Waiter Right, let's have a look. Yes, that's fine. And the name is?
Customer Lambeth, that's L-A-M-B-E-T-H.
Waiter Thanks, and could I just take a phone number?
Customer Yes, it's 554 2888.
Waiter Great. See you at 8.30, Mr Lambeth.

18 SATURDAY & SUNDAY

1

Bruce Hi, Vic. How was your weekend?
Vic Well, I came to the office on Saturday morning, but I had a great time after that.
Bruce What did you do?
Vic It was non-stop – tennis, pub, cinema …
Bruce What film did you see?
Vic *Go*. It was brilliant. Sarah didn't think so – she thought it was awful. Anyway … We went to the pub afterwards and met Alison. And she gave me a birthday present … for the first time! Why didn't you come with us? I told you about it.
Bruce I tried to phone you, but you weren't in. Karen came round for dinner.
Vic How did it go?
Bruce A disaster. I made fish pie but I left it in the oven too long. It didn't come out very well …
Vic Oh.
Bruce Then we had a row and Karen left early. Not a very good evening …

2

Part 1

Karen Hi there, Sarah.
Sarah Oh, hi. How was your weekend? How was the romantic dinner with Bruce?
Karen It wasn't a great success. I went round to his place, and he made dinner for me, but it was horrible. And then we had a row. In the end I left at about 9.30.
Sarah Oh dear.
Karen Yeah, well. What about you? What did you do?

Part 2

Sarah I went to the pictures with Vic. We saw a film called *Go*. I don't recommend it! Vic really liked it, but I thought it was terrible.
Karen Did you see Alison?

Sarah Yeah, we met her in the pub, and she gave Vic a CD for his birthday, so he was very pleased! Pity you weren't there …
Karen You can say that again …

3

opened
finished
started

19 TOWN & COUNTRY

1

Jan You're looking brown. Where've you been?
Lucy I've just got back from Australia and New Zealand.
Jan Wow! You lucky thing! How long were you there for?
Lucy Nearly a month altogether – the first two weeks in Australia, and then a week and a half in New Zealand.
Jan What was it like?
Lucy Absolutely fantastic. Australia was great – beautiful cities, brilliant night life, wonderful beaches, but a bit crowded …
Jan What was the weather like?
Lucy Sunny every day! It was *so* hot. I got sunburn the first day, and I needed factor 20 for days!
Jan Where did you stay?
Lucy Actually, in some very comfortable hotels, and they weren't expensive either.

2

Jan How about New Zealand?
Lucy New Zealand was much quieter than Australia. The countryside is a lot greener and more mountainous. Unfortunately it's a lot cloudier, too, but we thought it was more beautiful.
Jan 'We'? Who's 'we'?
Lucy Secret …

20 TICKETS & FLIGHTS

1

Part 1

Travel agent Hello, Timetravel, Andy speaking, how can I help you?
Ms McCall Oh hello, I'd like to book a flight, please.
Travel agent Where to?
Ms McCall To Barcelona.
Travel agent And when would you like to travel?
Ms McCall 15 June, if possible.
Travel agent And coming back?
Ms McCall The first of July.
Travel agent And how many people is that for?
Ms McCall Just me.
Travel agent OK, bear with me for a moment … We've got flights on the fifteenth at 08.20 arriving 10.50 and at 16.40 arriving 19.20.
Ms McCall The 08.20 would be good.
Travel agent And coming back on the first there's 09.00 arriving 11.15 or 15.15 arriving 17.50.
Ms McCall The 15.15, please.
Travel agent OK.
Ms McCall And could you tell me how much that is, please?
Travel agent Yes, sure. It'll be £90, which includes airport tax.
Ms McCall OK, that's fine.
Travel agent How would you like to pay?

Part 2

Travel agent How would you like to pay?
Ms McCall Visa, please.
Travel agent Could I have the number?
Ms McCall It's 4929 4781 3111.
Travel agent And the expiry date?
Ms McCall 07/06.
Travel agent And the holder's name?
Ms McCall RS McCall, that's M, small c, capital C, A, double L.
Travel agent Great. So that's a return to Barcelona, leaving 15 June 08.20, returning 1 July 15.15.
Ms McCall Yeah, that's right.
Travel agent OK. If I could give you a reference number. It's CT 12435. Please quote that number if you have any queries. Could you confirm your address and postcode?
Ms McCall Yes, it's 22 Castle Road, Edinburgh.
Travel agent And the postcode?
Ms McCall EH8 7DS.
Travel agent Fine. The ticket will be in the post – you should get it tomorrow.
Ms McCall Thanks, bye.
Travel agent Bye.

21 SINGLES & DOUBLES

1

Receptionist Hello, Hotel Excelsior.
David Yes, hello. I'd like to book a room for this Friday and Saturday, please.
Receptionist Certainly, sir, what kind of room would you like?
David A double room with en suite bathroom, please.
Receptionist Yes, we have a double free at $225 with breakfast.
David OK. Can I phone back later to confirm?
Receptionist Yes, that's fine.
David OK, thank you. Goodbye.
Receptionist Goodbye.

2

Receptionist Hello, the Majestic.
David Yes, hello. I'd like to book a double room with en suite bathroom for Friday and Saturday, please.
Receptionist I'm afraid all the en suite doubles are taken, sir. We can offer you two en suite singles.
David How much are the two singles?
Receptionist They're $90 each.
David Is that with breakfast?
Receptionist No, that's just the rooms.
David OK, thank you. I'll think about it. Goodbye.
Receptionist Goodbye.

3

Receptionist Hello, Hotel Excelsior.
David Yes, hello. I'd like to confirm a booking for this Friday and Saturday, please …

4

1 Do you have any rooms free for tomorrow night?
2 I'd like to book a double room for Friday and Saturday.
3 Can I phone back later to confirm?
4 How much is a single?
5 Is that with breakfast?
6 I'd like to confirm a booking, please.

22 WHEN & WHERE

🔊1

Alex Mark, have you ever been to Canada?

Mark Yeah, a few times. I went on a work trip to Toronto last year. Why?

Alex Well, I need your advice. I'm spending three weeks on holiday there next month, and I'm not sure about the best way to take money.

Mark I've always taken credit cards – you can use them everywhere, and you don't need to carry cash around.

Alex Have you ever lost them?

Mark Only once. I left my wallet on a table in a restaurant, and luckily the manager phoned my hotel.

Alex And what about traveller's cheques?

Mark I haven't used them for years. They're OK, and most hotels will change them, but you pay commission when you buy them, it's about 3% ...

Alex True. Yeah, it sounds as if credit cards would be best.

Mark Definitely. And maybe some cash, a few hundred dollars, for taxis and things ...

Alex OK, well, thanks for the advice.

Mark That's OK – have a good trip!

23 SHOPS & SHOPPING

🔊1

1 A I'd like some **travel sickness pills**, please.
  B We've got them in boxes of 12 or 24.

2 A Have you got this **jacket** in **extra large**?
  B Hold on, I'll just check for you.

3 A Could I try these **boots** on, please?
  B What size are you?
  A I think I'm a **39**.

4 A Have you got any English–**Spanish** dictionaries?
  B Yes, on the **third** floor.

5 A Could you tell me where the **bread** is?
  B Yes, it's in aisle **seven**.

6 A I'd like to send this **letter**, please.
  B First or second class?

7 A How would you like it?
  B Two **tens** and a **twenty**, please.

8 A Have you got any **French** newspapers?
  B No, sorry, we're sold out.

🔊2

1 Can I help you?
2 Do you mean a camera?
3 What's it called?
4 What are you looking for?
5 I don't know the word in English.
6 I wonder if you could help me, please.
7 Yes, that's it.
8 I don't know what it's called in English.

🔊3

1

Assistant Can I help you?

Customer Yes, I'm looking for something, but I don't know the word in English. It's for putting photographs in.

Assistant Oh, a photo frame.

Customer Yes, that's it.

2

Customer Hello. I wonder if you could help me, please.

Assistant Of course. What are you looking for?

Customer That's the problem – I don't know what it's called in English. It's for taking photographs.

Assistant Do you mean a camera?

Customer No, the thing in the camera. What's it called?

Assistant Oh, the film.

Customer Yes, that's it.

24 SUITS & BOOTS

🔊1

1 I'm not very sporty, but everyone wears them – they're just really comfortable.
2 I keep everything in it – keys, cheque book, driving licence, make-up, address book ... I'd be lost without it!
3 I hate having cold hands, so I really love them.
4 I prefer them to a skirt – much more practical, especially with all those pockets.
5 It's very light and very warm, but it lets the wind through and it isn't waterproof.

🔊2

1

Shop assistant Are you all right there?

Customer Just looking, thanks.

2

Shop assistant Can I help you?

Customer Yes, have you got these in a large?

3

Customer What do you think?

Friend It looks great.

4

Shop assistant Any good?

Customer Yeah, I'll take this one, please.

IRREGULAR VERBS

Infinitive	Past simple	Past participle
be	was / were	been
become	became	become
begin	began	begun
break	broke	broken
bring	brought	brought
build	built	built
buy	bought	bought
catch	caught	caught
choose	chose	chosen
come	came	come
cost	cost	cost
cut	cut	cut
do	did	done
draw	drew	drawn
drink	drank	drunk
drive	drove	driven
eat	ate	eaten
fall	fell	fallen
feel	felt	felt
find	found	found
fly	flew	flown
forget	forgot	forgotten
get	got	got
give	gave	given
go	went	gone
grow	grew	grown
have	had	had
hear	heard	heard
hit	hit	hit
hold	held	held
hurt	hurt	hurt
keep	kept	kept
know	knew	known
leave	left	left
lend	lent	lent

Infinitive	Past simple	Past participle
lose	lost	lost
make	made	made
mean	meant	meant
meet	met	met
pay	paid	paid
put	put	put
read	read	read
ride	rode	ridden
ring	rang	rung
run	ran	run
say	said	said
see	saw	seen
sell	sold	sold
send	sent	sent
shine	shone	shone
show	showed	shown
shut	shut	shut
sing	sang	sung
sit	sat	sat
sleep	slept	slept
speak	spoke	spoken
spend	spent	spent
stand	stood	stood
steal	stole	stolen
swim	swam	swum
take	took	taken
teach	taught	taught
tell	told	told
think	thought	thought
understand	understood	understood
upset	upset	upset
wake up	woke up	woken up
wear	wore	worn
win	won	won
write	wrote	written

Acknowledgements

The Publisher and Authors are grateful to those who have given permission to reproduce the following extracts and adaptations of copyright material:

p.26 Extracts from *Time Out* Magazine 2–9 February 2000. Reproduced by permission of *Time Out Magazine*.
p.53 Extracts from *Edinburgh The Best!* by Peter Irvine published by HarperCollins Publishers. Reproduced by permission of HarperCollins Publishers, Glasgow.
p.93 'Alarm Calls' and 'In an emergency call 999' from *The Phone Book*. Reproduced by permission of British Telecommunications PLC.
p.95 Extracts from *Russian: A Rough Guide Phrasebook*. Published by Rough Guides 1997. Reproduced by permission of Rough Guides.

Illustrations by:

Jonathan Clark p.09
Emma Dodd/Black Hat pp.36, 42, 56, 61, 80, 82, 92
Mark Duffin pp.05, 19, 29, 39, 67, 72, 85, 96, 100
Turinna Gren/Inkshed pp.13, 74
Hardlines pp.30, 89, 105, 106
Nanette Hoogslag/Debut Art cover image
Ian Jackson pp.38, 40, 41, 47, 75, 88
Maria Raymondsdotter p.50
Willie Ryan pp.15, 22, 64, 65, 66, 83, 91, 93, 102
Technical Graphics, OUP, pp.16, 17, 29, 58, 62, 78
Margaret Welbank pp.28, 79

Commissioned photography by:

Gareth Boden (styling by Diane Jones) pp.04, 55, 56, 71, 73, 76, 94
Mark Mason p.36 (bags)

The Publisher and Authors would like to thank the following for their kind permission to reproduce photographs:

Action Plus p.26 (Neil Tingle/basketball)
Bryan and Cherry Alexander pp.07 (Mali woman), 98 (Iceland)
Associated Press pp.70 (Danielle Smith/boutique), 102 (Jay Laprete)
John Birdsill pp.32 (man in paisley tie, man in black tie, girl)
Collections pp.37 (Geoff Howard/taxi), 52 (Roger Scruton/Mumtaz restaurant), 54 (Lawrence Englesberg/Rusholme Restaurant), 64 (Gill Jones/guest house), 65 (Julian Nieman/house, Michael St Maur Sheil/Cork)
Corbis Images pp.10 (Sheldan Collins/village), 25 (Araldo de Luca/pot, Phil Schermeister/place setting), 26 (Robbie Jack/Romeo and Juliet), 51 (Kevin Fleming), 54 (Peter Wilson/tapas)
Greg Evans p.08 (Italian woman), p.10 (Greek woman)
Will Forsyth and Sue Lavender p.16
Getty One Stone pp.07 (Scot Montgomery/Japanese girl), 08 (Ken Fisher/American man), 17 (Dale Durfee/woman in sunglasses), 23 (Paul Edmonson/man smiling, Ron Krisel/woman smiling, David Roth/woman smiling), 31 (Robert Stahl/lilies), 37 (John Lamb/bus, Martin Barraud/motorbike), 64 Ken Biggs/hotel, Alan Levenson/camper van)
Habitat p.36 (chair)
Hutchison Library p.17 (Edward Parker/Solomon Islands)
Image Bank pp.15 (Peter Till), 37 (Chris Close/coach, Lockyer Romilly/underground), 44 (Donata Pizzi/woman)
Katz Pictures pp.07 (Werner Gartung/Laif/Indian man, Elodie Gregoire/REA/Algerian woman), 11 (Fulvio Zanetini/girl), 37 (Chloe Fletcher/ferry), 52 (Richard Baker/businessmen eating, Mcdonald's, Ludovic/REA/pizza), 70 (Jean Francois Pin/Delicatessen)
Shawn Keys p.12 (Shawn)
Kobal Collection p.32 (programme)
Sue Kyes, Leo van Linh, and Mark Paine p.82
Diana and Jack Potten p.12 (Diana)

Press Association pp.25 (Fiona Hansen/Tate), 70 (Barry Batchelor/Asda Wal-Mart), 87 (EPA/Tate), 97 (Stefan Rousseau/party)
Robert Harding Picture Library pp.07 (J Strachan/old man), 11 (Ellen Rooney/Athens), 25 (International Stock/coffee, V Skeet/disco ball, panda, Paul Reeves/beer, masks), 31 (dancers), 34 (pizza, Eurostar), 36 (umbrella), 37 (train, car, aeroplane), 44 (N Penny/MR/businessman), 54 (Chinatown), 59 (hills), 64 (G Renner/campsite), 66 (Fraser Hall), 69 (white-water rafting), 98 (Saudi Arabia, Greece, Argentina, Tanzania, R Francis/Russia, Gavin Hellier/China, Australia)
Ronald Grant Archive p.25 (Titanic)
Still Moving Picture Company pp.46 (Doug Corrance/The Italian Centre), 52 (Doug Corrance/L'Aubage), 54 (Doug Corrance/Rogano Restaurant), 104 (Ken Paterson/dancer, SJ Taylor/detail)
Telegraph Colour Library pp.31 (Ron Chapple/promenade), 59 (PI Productions/Sydney bridge)
Trip pp.05 (T Why), 26 R Cracknell/Museum), 52 (S Grant/two women), 64 (S Grant/cooking)

The Publisher would like to thank Faith and Shannon Hill for their time and assistance.

The Publisher and Authors would like to thank the following for their feedback on the course:

Catherine Bond (freelance)
David and Emma Illsley (freelance)
Alison McKnight (Edinburgh School of English)
Russell Stannard (freelance)

Heather and Jonathan would like to thank the teachers of the Edinburgh School of English who offered their ideas and comments, and all the students who helped pilot those ideas. Special thanks to Junko for her drawing. Thanks also to our neighbours and the students at Edinburgh's Telford College for giving up their time to be interviewed. Finally, a big thank you to Alison for her observations and suggestions.